Read Faster,
Recall More

Books to change your life and work.
Accessible, easy to read and easy to act on –
Other titles in the **How To** series include:

Improving Your Written English
How to ensure your grammar, punctuation and spelling are up to scratch

Polish Up Your Punctuation and Grammar
Master the basics of the English language and write with greater confidence

Passing Exams Without Anxiety
How to get organised, be prepared and feel confident of success

Critical Thinking for Students
How to assess arguments and effectively present your own

Maximising Your Memory
How to train yourself to remember more

The **How To** series now contains
around 200 titles in the following categories:

Business & Management
Career Choices
Career Development
Computers & the Net
Creative Writing
Home & Family
Living & Working Abroad
Personal Development
Personal Finance
Self-Employment & Small Business
Study Skills & Student Guides

For full details, please send for a free copy
of the latest catalogue to:

How To Books
3 Newtec Place, Magdalen Road
Oxford OX4 1RE, United Kingdom
e-mail: info@howtobooks.co.uk
http://www.howtobooks.co.uk

Read Faster, Recall More

*Use proven techniques for speed
reading and maximum recall*

GORDON WAINWRIGHT

How To Books

Published by How To Books Ltd,
3 Newtec Place, Magdalen Road,
Oxford OX4 1RE, United Kingdom.
Tel: (01865) 793806. Fax: (01865) 248780.
email: info@howtobooks.co.uk
http://www.howtobooks.co.uk

First edition 2001

British Library Cataloguing in Publication Data.
A catalogue record for this book is available from
the British Library.

Edited by Julie Nelson
Cover design by Shireen Nathoo Design
Cover image by PhotoDisc

Produced for How To Books by Deer Park Productions
Typeset by Kestrel Data, Exeter
Printed and bound by Cromwell Press Ltd, Trowbridge, Wiltshire

NOTE: The material contained in this book is set out in good
faith for general guidance and no liability can be accepted
for loss or expense incurred as a result of relying in particular
circumstances on statements made in the book. Laws and
regulations are complex and liable to change, and readers should
check the current position with the relevant authorities before
making personal arrangements.

Contents

1

The Starting Point

Before you begin the process of improving your reading skills, you need to know where you are starting from. Reading performance is traditionally measured purely in terms of comprehension, but most people want to be able to deal with their daily reading faster and yet recall it effectively when required. Neither of these is assessed in school comprehension tests, yet good recall is essential for better comprehension. A prerequisite for achieving this is to find out what your reading speeds and recall levels are before you begin trying some new techniques. This chapter is therefore devoted to assessing the starting point for this programme of training.

READING SPEED AND POST-READING RECALL

Before you begin working through this book and before you succumb to the temptation to look ahead and see what is coming, you should measure your present reading speed and post-reading recall. It is important to measure the latter because, if recall is not good immediately after reading something, it is not likely to improve later. You will find two exercises in the following pages that will enable you to do this, together with instructions on precisely how to complete them.

You should tackle these exercises as soon as possible because if you are tempted to look ahead at the rest of this book, this may influence the way in which you approach them and prevent you from finding out how good your reading skills were before you picked this book up.

Your reading performance will be tested and recorded by working through two exercises, taking an average of your results and then marking these on the progress graphs on page 120. As you read these exercises, you should try to read them as quickly as you feel you can and still take the information in. You want, after all, to see how quickly you can read before you try new techniques.

When you come to answering the questions of the recall tests, you should avoid guessing answers if you do not know them. If you guess the answers, you may be right and this will make you think your recall is better than it really is.

For the same reason, you should not try to 'spot' questions, that is, try as you read to memorise isolated bits of information on the off chance that they may be required. They may, of course, but if they are then all you have proved is that you are a good 'spotter'. You have not proved to yourself that you have taken in what you have read. You will be the only person who knows how well or how badly you are doing, so why try to delude yourself? You will be much better off in the long run if you are as honest with yourself as it is possible to be. That way you will know accurately whether or not you have improved and by how much.

THE STRUCTURE OF THE PROGRAMME

This programme consists of five stages:

1. **Review of present performance** – finding out where your starting point is.

2. **Objective setting** – deciding what you wish to achieve by working through the programme.

3. **Methods** – exploring the various methods for bringing about improvement and finding which ones work best for you.

4. **Evaluation of improved performance** – finding out how much you have improved by the end of the programme.

5. **Ongoing** – learning what you will need to do to maintain your improvements and to continue your development as a more efficient reader.

THE FIRST STAGE

The procedure for the first stage of the process is as follows:

- You read each passage once only as quickly as you can take it in and time the reading (for this you will need a stopwatch, watch with a timer or a watch with a second hand).

- You answer the recall test, remembering not to guess if you do not know the answer nor to try to work the answer out.

- You convert the reading time into words per minute (using the conversion table on pages 119–120), check the answers to the recall test against the answers on pages 121–122 and record both results on the progress graphs on page 120.

Make sure you have your timing device ready and a pen or pencil for recording your answers.

If you are using a stopwatch or watch with a timer, follow your handbook's instructions for timing an event. If you are using a watch with a second hand, make a note of the time in minutes and seconds when you start. This is easier if you wait until the second hand is pointing to 12. Make a note of the time when you finish and then subtract the starting time from the finishing time.

EXERCISE

Start timing and begin reading NOW.

One of Our Tankers Is Missing

'You can't be serious,' Henry Clough told his assistant James Wright.

'It's true,' James affirmed.

'But a tanker. You can't lose a tanker. Not one with all the latest nautical technology at its disposal,' Henry protested.

'You wouldn't think so,' agreed James, 'but it's gone. Last reported in the Atlantic at 2330 last night. Since then, nothing. No reports. No Mayday. Nothing. We've contacted all vessels known to be in the area at the time and none of them has any record of seeing it or having it on radar after 2330.'

Henry looked thoughtful for a few moments.

'No storms, I suppose,' he ventured.

'No, the weather was pretty good. A large swell and strongish winds, but nothing that would worry the *Lady Lavinia*. She was as you know one of our most advanced vessels. Only been in service for two years. Only been in port and checked over last month. It's a complete mystery.'

'We'd better tell the boss,' concluded Henry.

They took the lift to the top floor and walked along the luxurious corridor to the managing director's suite.

Fortunately, he was free and they were ushered in straight away. They told their story to an increasingly incredulous Sebastian Shorofski.

There was a long silence when they had finished. Eventually, the big man spoke.

'Treat this as suspicious and instigate a full search and rescue. It could just be that she has for some reason suffered a total and catastrophic loss of all systems and is drifting helplessly out there somewhere.'

Henry and James went back to Henry's office and began the lengthy procedure of initiating and co-ordinating the search.

At Mr Shorofski's request, the media were not informed. He decided it was best not to alarm families and friends of the crew unnecessarily. After all, the tanker could reappear just as mysteriously as it had disappeared.

The search continued for several days without success, but on the Friday of that week an RAF Nimrod thought it sighted what looked like a very large oil slick off the coast of Ireland. If the oil came ashore it would be a bigger environmental disaster than the *Exxon Valdiz* off the coast of Alaska some years previously.

'We really ought to issue some sort of statement,' said Henry Clough anxiously. 'No,' said Shorofski firmly. 'Not until the loss of the ship is confirmed. It may not be our oil.'

'But the authorities will need time to organise mopping up operations,' protested Clough. 'If it emerges later that we knew about this slick, even if it isn't ours, and didn't tell anyone, we'll be crucified in the media. We could even face criminal charges.'

Shorofski was adamant. 'The RAF spotted it – or thought they did – let them tell people. There's no reason at this stage for us to get involved. For goodness' sake, we don't even know yet for definite that there is an oil slick. You panic too quickly, Henry.'

Henry Clough looked glumly out of the window. He knew from past experience that there was no arguing with Sebastian Shorofski once he had made up his mind. Nevertheless, he hardly slept that night and was not at all looking forward to going into work the next day, but he had to have another try with Shorofski.

(556 words)

Stop timing and make a note of the time and answer the following questions *without looking back at the passage.*

Questions
1. What was the name of Henry Clough's assistant?

2. At what time was the last report received from the tanker?

3. What was the name of the tanker.

4. For how long had the tanker been in service?

5. What was Sebastian Shorofski's position in the company?

6. What was his initial reaction to being told of the tanker's disappearance?

7. Off the coast of which country was the suspected oil slick sighted?

8. What was the weather like when the tanker disappeared?

9. When had the tanker last been in port?

10. On which day of the week did the RAF Nimrod think it had spotted an oil slick?

Convert the reading time into words per minute (using the conversion table on pages 119–120), check the answers to the recall test against the answers on pages 121–122 and record both results on the progress graphs on page 120.

You should, then, have finished up with a speed in words per minute and a recall score out of ten (converted into a percentage by placing 0 after your score, e.g. 7 out of 10=70%, there is a reason for doing this which will be explained in Chapter 5). Make sure you have recorded this on vertical line 1 or in the column to the left of line 1 on the comprehension graph, depending on whether you wish to build up a graph or a bar chart. Either method will produce a picture which develops as you proceed and will later enable you to see where you are, where you have come from and where you might be likely to finish up. It thus provides you with both instant and cumulative feedback on your performance.

EXERCISE

Begin timing the second exercise and begin reading NOW.

If You're Going Back to San Francisco

We've all heard the publicist's claim, 'This is Everybody's Favourite City.' Well, it's certainly mine. I first went there about ten years ago, just before companies began seriously to look at the expense of sending their executives first class on long-haul journeys. I had been to America before, of course, but that was to Florida. This was very different. It was about twenty degrees cooler and the humidity in comparison was negligible.

What pleased me most, I think, apart from the skyline, was that it was a city you could walk about in and actually feel that in half an hour or so you were getting somewhere. We went to all the usual tourist spots – the Coit Tower, Lombard Street ('the crookedest street in the world' with its succession of hairpin bends), the Embarcadero and Fisherman's Wharf.

The Wharf was a delight, not for the crowds, but for the fact that Earthquake McGoon's was still open at the time and Turk Murphy's Jazz Band were playing. I even bought one of his cassettes and had him autograph it. I still play it when nostalgia overtakes me.

We had a car while we were there as we intended to visit companies in the surrounding area and on one free afternoon we drove across the Golden Gate Bridge, my favourite piece of architecture not least because it was opened in the year I was born. We drove up Highway One into Muir Woods and stopped at the Pelican Inn near Muir Beach. This is a passable imitation, certainly for America, of a sixteenth-century English inn. We had sausage and mash and a pint of Bass. By US standards, it was expensive, but when you've been away from home for a while you get homesick. After drinking their lager-like beers, it was a genuine refreshment to quaff proper beer. It was so good we had another.

The next time I went to San Francisco, I was left on my own for a few days as my colleage had to return early. This time I drove south down Highway One. I followed the coast as far as Santa Cruz and then headed inland. I was looking for a small town we had held a meeting in on the first visit,

Los Altos, not far from Palo Alto. I found it without much difficulty and strolled around its pleasantly warm streets, even though this was October, and found an incredibly good bookshop. It has always puzzled me that bookshops in America often have a far wider choice of books than even some of the better bookshops in British towns and cities. I found a quiet bar and had a beer. The atmosphere of US small towns can be so relaxing and it is surprising how much the pace of life slows down even when only a few miles away from a conurbation.

The last time I was in San Francisco was with my wife and we found it a disappointment. We were flying round the world to celebrate our silver wedding anniversary. This time they city was cold and damp and my wife yearned for the Hawaii and the Bali we had recently departed. It was to get even worse in New York and I think she was secretly pleased to get back home.

On the Wharf, Earthquake McGoon's was gone. I could not even find a sign anywhere of its existence. When we went to Alioto's for a fish dinner, the lady who served us came from a small town no more than ten miles away from where we live. It felt as if we weren't really abroad. It was like some years earlier on my first visit to Japan. We had finished business for the day in Kobe and were taken by one of the British officials to a bar for a drink before going out for dinner. There was only one other person in the bar at the time, a Geordie engineer. Again, I almost felt cheated. It was as if, so far away from home, no one else from your own country had the right to intrude.

I'd like to go back to San Francisco, but then again I'm not so sure. They do say that, in life, you should never go back. Things are never the same. They certainly weren't on the Wharf.

(725 words)

Stop timing and make a note of the time and answer the following questions *without looking back at the passage.*

Questions

1. How does the publicist's claim describe San Francisco?

2. Which state had the writer visited before his first visit to San Francisco?

3. What was the name of the jazz band that was playing at Earthquake McGoon's?

4. What was the name of the replica of a sixteenth-century English inn?

5. What was the brand of beer the writer drank there?

6. On which highway did the writer drive on both visits?

7. How far south did he drive on his second visit?

8. What was the name of the small town he visited on the second trip?

9. What did he find in this town that was incredibly good?

10. Who was the only other occupant of the bar in Kobe, Japan?

Convert the reading time into words per minute (using the conversion table on pages 119–120), check the answers to the recall test against the answers on pages 121–122 andrecord both results on the progress graphs on page 120.

Now average the two results for both speed and recall and make a note of them.

ASSESSMENT OF RESULTS

Typically, at this stage, reading speed averaged over the two exercises is somewhere between 150 words per minute (w.p.m.) and 250 w.p.m. An average recall score is about 50–70%. This may not seem very high, but I can assure you that in my experience these are average figures at this point.

There is no evidence of any correlation between reading speed and intelligence, age, education, occupation or anything else. Many highly intelligent people, for example, are very slow readers, especially if they have had large amounts of study reading to deal with. Nor is there much evidence of a correlation between recall and any of these factors. So, don't worry if your results are on the low side. This simply means there is more to be gained from the programme.

THE NEXT STEP

Now that you have some idea of where you are starting from, it is time to begin to work through the programme. What you will be doing is based on the simple fact that there are people who are quite naturally faster and more efficient readers than others. Research over the years has identified many of the techniques they use. You will be given the opportunity to try them out and see which ones work best for you. The programme aims to achieve improvement in reading skills by:

- developing appropriate attitudes towards reading

- undertaking a programme of work designed to raise maximum speeds in reading

- developing systematic approaches to handling written materials.

You are now ready to move on to stage two of the programme which you should attempt whenever you feel ready. You may prefer to have a rest at this point and resume tomorrow. You will find stage two in Chapter 2 and you are now free to browse through the rest of this book should you wish. You should not look too closely at any of the exercises, though, as they will then not provide you with the right kind of test at the appropriate time.

FURTHER PRACTICE

You will find it helps a great deal if you carry out the following tasks before proceeding:

- Measure your reading speed on a variety of the kinds of materials you normally have to deal with. Do not try to do it too precisely as an estimate of the number of words read will suffice. You should still be able to calculate reading speed with reasonable accuracy. Two simple methods of estimating the number of words read are:

  - Count the number of words in 10 lines and divide by 10 to obtain an average per line. Multiply this by the number of lines on a typical page. Then multiply this by the number of pages read.

– Measure off 1" (one inch) of text (a centimetre is not enough). Count the number of words. Multiply this by the length of the piece in column or page inches.

Test recall by noting down briefly what you remember from each piece.

- Make a list of the different kinds of materials you have to deal with together with an assessment of how important it is to retain information read for each one.

- Read at least one item purely for the pleasure of reading it (a chapter of a novel, an article of special interest or a chapter of a book on a subject of particular interest to you personally). You may, of course, read more than the specified amount if you wish. The more widely you read from now on, the better. It will not be a question of, 'Never mind the quality, feel the width', though. Variety is more important than mere quantity.

CHAPTER SUMMARY

In this chapter you have learned:

- how to measure your reading speed
- how to test your recall of information
- the structure of the programme
- your starting point for the programme
- how to complete the first of the five stages of the programme.

2

Aims and Objectives

SETTING YOUR TARGETS

Now that you have completed the first stage of the programme and you know your starting point, you need to decide where you want to go. How big an increase in reading speed do you want? How much improvement in recall do you want or need? Based on more than thirty years' experience in training people to read faster and better, I would suggest you set yourself the following targets:

- 100% increase in reading speed

- a recall level of at least 70%.

The increase in reading speed may seem high, but I have seen many people achieve it and some have gone even further. Set your targets low and your final results will be low. Set them too high and you may well be disappointed. 100% is reasonable because most people have never had any training in increasing reading speeds. It is not something that school or college teachers normally concern themselves with. There is therefore a gap between what has been achieved and what could be achieved. Here, you are about to bridge that gap.

Now, mark those two targets on the progress graphs on page 120. In this way you will be reminded of your basic objectives every time you record results on the graphs. This will help you to move towards them.

OTHER AIMS AND OBJECTIVES

You may, of course, have other aims and objectives which you wish to achieve. You may, for instance, wish to improve other aspects of your comprehension in addition to recall. You may want to increase your flexibility in dealing with different kinds of materials. You may wish to become a more critical reader, where critical means not just looking for faults but trying to identify points of merit as well in order to reach a balanced judgement about a piece of writing. You may even set yourself the aim of broadening your reading interests and selecting both your work-related and leisure reading from a wider range of sources.

Whatever additional aims and objectives you have, you will find it useful to write them down in the space below:

1. Critical reader

2.

3.

4.

5.

6.

Use a separate sheet of paper if you have more than six. Try to make a distinction, if you can, between aims and objectives. An **aim** will tell you the direction in which you wish to proceed; an **objective** will tell you how far you want to go in that direction. Objectives are more useful because they are more precise and quantifiable and they should be expressed as results to be achieved. It is therefore easier to check later how far you have succeeded.

A LIFELONG PROCESS

That completes stage two of the programme. In the next chapter, we shall begin to explore stage three and see what techniques may help you to reach your targets. This comprises the bulk of what follows in the book. Towards the end, we shall see how much improvement you have made and the book will end with techniques for continuing and following up on your progress in the future. Reading improvement, like education itself, can be a lifelong process.

EXERCISE

Before you turn to the next chapter, complete the next exercise. As you read, try to read faster than you have so far. You can, in fact, increase your reading speed by 20-30% simply by trying without using any new techniques. You might as well have the benefit of this before we look at other techniques. So, get into the habit of **competing with yourself**. Try to achieve a 'new personal best' on each exercise. Whilst there is little point in competing with other people, because they will most likely have started at a different speed and may not progress at the same rate as you, there is every point in a little healthy self-competition and self-pacing to move gradually closer to your objectives.

Begin timing and start reading NOW.

The Great Cash Register Mystery

Hobson's was not a busy shop, but trade had always been steady. Turnover was enough to keep Mr and Mrs Hobson in reasonable comfort and provide employment for three part-time assistants. The Hobsons had bought the little general dealer's when Mr Hobson had taken early retirement from the accountancy firm where he had worked for nearly thirty years.

The assistants were all pleasant girls, popular with the locals who dropped in mainly to buy things they had forgotten to get at the supermarket or had just run out of and couldn't be bothered to get the car out to go to the out-of-town shopping mall. Jane was the oldest, 19, married with a young baby who was looked after by her mother when she was working at the shop. Susan was 17, rather on the plump side, unmarried and usually without a boy friend. Gina was 16, fresh from school, slim, very attractive and with more boy friends than you could shake a stick at.

Life at the shop was uneventful to say the least until the day Mrs Hobson, when totalling the day's receipts, found a discrepancy. It was not a large amount, £1.20, but sufficiently irritating to the meticulous Mrs Hobson for her to mention it to Mr Hobson. He checked her arithmetic and the till receipts and came to the same conclusion. They were £1.20 short.

Many people, of course, would be more than happy if they were only that much short on the day, but Mr Hobson's accountancy background did not permit him to take such a cavalier attitude. They would have to make sure that it did not happen again.

But it did happen again. The next week on the same day, Thursday, they were £1.20 down again. They checked and re-checked, but the deficit stubbornly refused to go away.

On the first occasion they had said nothing to the three girls, but this time they did ask if anyone had felt they might inadvertently have given someone too much change. The girls were quite sure they had not. The mystery remained.

The following week they were £1.20 down on Tuesday as well as Thursday. The week after they were £1.20 down again on Tuesday and Thursday. Something would have to be done.

Mr Hobson had a friend who was a television engineer and when the problem was explained to him he fixed a closed circuit television camera to observe the till. When they viewed the recordings, they could see nothing to explain the deficit.

The solution to the mystery came quite unexpectedly. Susan was ringing in a customer's purchases when the drawer of the till stuck. No matter what she did, she could not get it to close. When Mr Hobson dismantled the till, he found the missing coins behind the drawer. It appeared that the spring clip on the till had somehow tightened and when it was shut it had propelled a coin forward and over the back of the drawer.

But why it had happened with such regularity and why always the same amount, no one was able to explain.

(521 words)

Stop timing and answer the following questions *without looking back at the passage.*

Questions

1. What was Mr Hobson's profession before he retired?
2. What was the name of the plump girl?
3. What kind of shop did the Hobsons run?
4. How much was the till short on each occasion?
5. How was life at the shop described?
6. What was the occupation of Mr Hobson's friend?
7. How was the till observed?
8. Where was the missing money found?
9. What had caused the money to go missing?
10. Who discovered the missing money?

Convert the reading time into words per minute (using the conversion table on pages 119–120), check the answers to the recall test against the answers on pages 121–122 and record both results on the progress graphs on page 120.

ASSESSMENT OF RESULTS

You should have found that this exercise was a little faster than the previous ones. If it was, all is well. If it was not, ask yourself if you were really trying. Could you have put a little more effort into it? You may, of course, be worried that greater speed will mean poorer recall. It may – at first. After all, you are being asked to do things in different ways from those you are used to. Once you do get used to them, many problems will solve themselves. If not, there should be techniques you will learn later in the programme that will be a help. Nothing you will be asked to do will cause permanent brain damage. You will always have the option at any point to go back to reading as you did before you started. Techniques that do not work the first time you try them may well do so at the third or fourth attempt. You simply need to get used to doing things differently. Persevere.

FURTHER PRACTICE

Continue the practice suggested at the end of Chapter 1.

CHAPTER SUMMARY

In this chapter you have learned:

- how to set objectives
- how to mark them on the progress graphs
- that it is desirable to have additional aims and objectives
- the difference between an aim and an objective
- the need for self-competition and self-pacing
- the need to try to read faster
- that it is important to persevere with the programme.

3

Basic Methods for Improvement

STAGE THREE

We now begin the third stage of the programme, which comprises the bulk of what follows in this book. You will be asked to try out a range of techniques and see which ones work best for you.

So far you already have in place techniques for timing, testing and recording what you do, which will provide you with continuous and cumulative feedback on what you do.

You have set objectives for achievement, the mere fact of doing which will tend to draw you towards them. That is why we set objectives for many activities in life and at work.

We have put in place the ideas of self-competition and self-pacing. Try to improve, but do so at your own pace. Do not try too hard, otherwise you may find that you are trying so hard that it actually gets in the way of making progress. Developing mental skills is not like developing physical skills where the advice 'no pain, no gain' is often given. Research shows that if you try too hard with a mental skill like reading you perform less well than if you learn to relax a little.

SETTING TIME LIMITS

We might now usefully introduce the idea of setting time limits for reading. When you have a chapter of a book or an article to read, use your developing awareness of your speeds for various materials to set **deadlines** for when you wish to have the reading completed. Writers find deadlines very useful and the same can be said for readers. As Dr Johnson once said, 'If a man knows that he is to be hanged in a fortnight, it concentrates the mind wonderfully.' You will not be hanged if you do not read faster, but the deadline will help you in your quest for progress.

Don't worry if you do not meet your deadlines at this stage. They are simply devices for encouraging you to look forwards in your reading rather than back. We shall return to this point in the exercise at the end of this chapter.

It might be worth pointing out here that all the techniques that we have encountered so far, as well as the others later in this chapter, are helpful in improving any skill, not just reading. The overall structure of the programme will also help to improve any skill. You always need to know your starting point, to set objectives, to have techniques for improvement available, to assess your progress after a reasonable period and have strategies for continuing the programme for as long as you want.

BEING MOTIVATED AND CONFIDENT

There are several other factors that can assist your progress. It helps, for instance, if you are **motivated** and actively want to improve. I have not mentioned it before because it seems reasonable to assume that if you are working through this programme you are already fairly highly motivated. Lack of motivation will not prevent you from making some improvement if you do all that is required of you in this book. An open mind, though, would be better than a negative attitude. Most progress will nevertheless be made if you have a **positive mental attitude** or PMA, as it is sometimes called.

It will also help if you approach the work with a certain amount of **confidence**. I am not asking you to say, 'Yes! I can do it!' All I am asking is that you think it might at least be possible. Three things may help to provide some confidence. As you progress, this may well give you the confidence to believe that you can go further. If you look at results others have achieved, this may persuade you to believe that, if others can do it, so can you. Nobody comes to the programme with two heads or three eyeballs. All are ordinary people in ordinary occupations where they need to get through paperwork quicker and more effectively.

Thirdly, there is the **training gap** we in effect encountered earlier, the fact that most people are taught how to read in primary school and then receive no further actual training in techniques of rapid reading and recall.

DO YOU NEED YOUR EYESIGHT CHECKING?

One final point might be worth making. When did you last have an eye test? If you have not had one in the last three years, it might be worth having your eyesight checked. Research shows that, when tested, 30% of people attending courses in reading improvement needed spectacles, at least for reading. Of those who were already wearing glasses, a further 30% needed new ones. If all this achieves is a slightly better and sharper contrast between the print and the paper it will make reading easier and therefore very likely faster. You have to remember that once you're over seventeen, it's all downhill.

EXERCISE

Now try the following exercise and as you read have a time limit in mind for when you would like to finish. Do not keep looking at your watch or timer to see whether or not you are going to make it. This will only slow you down. Just see how close you can get to a realistic deadline which will give you a little improvement on your best speed and recall score so far. Do not be disappointed if you do not achieve it at the first attempt. As with all the techniques in this book, you will become more used to them and more successful in using them with practice.

Start timing and begin reading NOW.

The Right Person
CFX plc had a problem. Morale was low. Staff turnover was high. Nobody knew what was wrong. But everybody knew that something was wrong and that something would have to be done about it. The question, however, was what?

One suggestion was to bring in a firm of consultants to study the problem and make recommendations. The managing director was not in favour of that idea, fearing that they might conclude that he was at fault. He preferred first of all to see if they could find a solution in-house. He summoned his Head of Personnel.

'What is the problem, John?' he asked.

'Well, sir, that's fairly easy. People are just not happy here. They do not get on with each other. It seems that every time we appoint somebody we seem to have a knack of selecting square pegs.'

The managing director sighed and said, 'Well, we have to do something. We can't go on like this otherwise the board are going to notice and start asking awkward questions. Last quarter's figures are already going to raise some eyebrows on faces I'd prefer to keep happy. Get your people to start from square one and see if they can find out where we're going wrong.'

The personnel director called his senior team members together and put the situation to them.

'We have got to come up with a solution,' he concluded.

They all sat silent for a full minute and then the newest recruit shuffled in his chair. They all turned to look at him expectantly. He reddened and looked uncomfortable.

'Well,' he began, 'You've all been here for some time. I only started two months ago.'

'So?' asked the deputy director of personnel.

'Well,' stumbled the newcomer, looking at her with a mixture of embarrassment and apprehension, 'I think there's something not quite right with our selection procedures.'

There was a general gasp of astonishment.

'We use a combination of interviews, the latest assessment tests and practical tests,' scorned the deputy director.

'I know, but we use the same procedure for every job. I think some people are getting through because they are good actors, because they are already familiar with the test or because the practical tests we use are not always appropriate to the job they are applying for.'

'What do you mean?' demanded the deputy director.

'Take my own case. I've always been good at interviews. I've practised in front of a video camera, with feedback from friends, and our interviews are typically only about thirty minutes long, regardless of the level of the job. I was more than familiar with the tests and had practised on them extensively. My practical test was to repair a broken typewriter. That's not really a relevant skill to my job as assistant training officer and, besides, my father used to run a second-hand office equipment business and I used to help him out in school holidays and university vacations.'

'So what do you think we should do?' asked the director.

At that moment the bell rang for the usual Thursday morning fire practice drill.

(521 words)

Stop timing and make a note of the time and answer the following questions *without looking back at the passage.*

Questions

1. What was the name of the company?

2. What was the first suggested solution to the problem?

3. Why did the managing director not favour this idea?

4. Whom did he summon to discuss the problem?

5. What were going to raise some eyebrows?

6. Who spoke first when the personnel director put the problem to his senior team members?

7. How long had this person worked for the company?

8. What event ended the meeting?

9. Name two of the techniques the company was currently using in staff selection.

10. What was the newcomer's practical test when interviewed for his job?

Convert the reading time into words per minute (using the conversion table on pages 119–120), check the answers to the recall test against the answers on pages 121–122 and record both results on the progress graphs on page 120.

ASSESSMENT OF RESULTS

Did you find the time limit helpful? If not, do some of the further practice in using time limits set out in the Further Practice section below.

If it did not work, don't despair. Remember our watchword: persevere. Always try things a few times before you give up on them.

FURTHER PRACTICE

Set time limits for a variety of pieces of writing. A good source of practice material for this programme lies in your 'Ought to Read' pile on your desk. I'm sure you have one. Most people do – items that should be read but rarely if ever are. Now you can kill two birds with one stone: fulfil the requirement for further practice and reduce the size of the pile.

CHAPTER SUMMARY

In this chapter you have learned:

- the need to continue using techniques already in place
- the value of time limits or deadlines for reading tasks
- the role of motivation in training skills
- the need to develop confidence in using the techniques
- the desirability of having regular eye tests.

4

The Mechanics of Reading

It will help at this point to learn a little about the nature of the reading process and be aware of what is actually happening as you are reading. We shall also look at the fourteen main differences between inefficient and efficient readers and see how we can improve our skills in each of these areas.

HOW YOUR EYES MOVE WHEN YOU ARE READING

Most people believe that when they are reading their eyes move smoothly along a line of print, but this is not the case. If you stand at a window overlooking a busy road and watch a car pass you from left to right, your eyes appear to move smoothly because they are focused on the car. In fact, they move in a very rapid series of small jerks, or **saccades** as they are called.

If you try to watch an imaginary car as it passes, anyone who watches your eyes will tell you that these saccades are larger and therefore visible. Watch someone's eyes over the top of a book or newspaper and you will see them clearly, but do pick someone you know, not strangers in pubs, for obvious reasons.

This is how the eyes move when you are reading. It is in the pauses or **fixations** between saccades that the reading is done. Research has shown that there is a mechanism in the brain which switches vision off 40 milliseconds before the eyes move and does not switch it completely back on again until 40 milliseconds after they have stopped moving. The amount you read at each fixation depends upon your span of perception or **eye span**.

Using your eye span

What all this means in practical terms is that, in order to increase your reading speed, you have to learn to space these fixations out more. Most slow readers read every word and yet you only have to look at a word to realise that you see more than one word at a time. Try it now. Focus on the dot above the i in the last sentence. Without moving your eyes, you will usually be able to see not just the word 'it', but also the word to the left and the word to the right. You will also be able to see the words above and below. You may even be able to see more than this. Whatever you can see without moving your eyes is your available eye span. Clearly, reading one word at a time is a wasteful use of resources.

CHARACTERISTICS OF THE MATURE READER: MECHANICAL DIFFERENCES

Research into reading in the United States has, in fact, identified fourteen characteristics of 'the mature reader'. We'll begin by looking at mechanical or physiological differences.

Regressing

The biggest problem that the inefficient or slow reader (the two are usually synonymous) has is that he or she **regresses**, that is, goes back to read things again. Most of us believe that these regressions are necessary because we do not understand the first time what we are being told. The evidence is, however, that this is normally not the case.

We go back for many other reasons. There is nothing to stop us going back, though when we are listening to information being given to us we rarely do it. When was the last time you asked a speaker to repeat the last few minutes of what they were saying? We regress to check that we have the information we need or should be getting. We regress out of lack of confidence. We regress out of habit. Yet the evidence is that, if you put people in a position in which they cannot regress, the loss of comprehension is on average no more than 3% to 7% and even this is recovered with a little bit of practice. We shall return later in this chapter to a simple technique which will enable us to avoid regressions.

Vocalising and inner speech

Many people vocalise or subvocalise as they read. **Vocalising** is simply a technical term for reading aloud. Some are unable to read silently. More subvocalise, that is, they read aloud silently. It is often called **inner speech** and is most noticeable if you are reading something written by someone you know well or by a well-known personality. It is as if you can 'hear' their voice as you read and it used to be regarded as a fault which had to be cured.

It is now not so seriously regarded for two reasons. No one has yet identified a cure for it and if you cannot cure a problem you simply have to live with it. More usefully, the Medical Research Council's Applied Psychology Unit at Cambridge University in England, which has done quite a lot of research into reading over the years, discovered that it was possible for people to read aloud at up to 475 words per minute and still understand what they were reading. I don't say people listening could understand, but the readers could understand. Presumably silent reading would permit even higher speeds because you would no longer be restricted by how quickly you could move your mouth muscles.

Most authorities put the limit on silent reading speed at about 800 words per minute (w.p.m.), though it may take some time to achieve this. My own top speed is about 600 w.p.m. and about 70% recall, but I have seen many people achieve higher speeds with even better comprehension. The best advice to give if you feel subvocalisation is a problem is to try to forget about it. It becomes less and less noticeable once you can achieve speeds in excess of 300 w.p.m.

Fixation time
Speed of perception or fixation time is a difference between slow and fast readers. There is not much you can do about this because you cannot control what you do in terms of fractions of seconds. It tends to become faster anyway with higher speeds, so it is another problem which takes care of itself.

Eye span
The same is true of eye span, which we mentioned earlier. Once you are operating at speeds above 300 w.p.m. you tend quite naturally to take in information in terms of groups of words rather than single words. There are, however, three techniques for you to try in this regard later in this chapter.

Rhythm
The slow reader, for fairly obvious reasons if much regression is taking place, lacks rhythm in reading. The faster reader has rhythmic, confident eye movements. The only backward movement is at the end of a line when moving to the beginning of the next line.

Flexible speeds

The slow reader also tends to read slowly all the time, no matter what he or she is reading. That is simply because he or she has no choice. The faster reader has a choice and can be flexible, reading easy materials quickly and demanding material relatively slowly, after skimming first. We shall return to skimming techniques in Chapter 9.

PSYCHOLOGICAL DIFFERENCES

Tension

Many slow readers experience tension when reading under pressure, for instance, when time is short. The efficient reader remains relaxed, even when reading against the clock.

Anticipating

Slow readers often have difficulty in anticipating the nature of subsequent material and tend to forget what they have read at the top of a page before they get to the bottom. This is because they are going so slowly that the impression made by earlier information fades before it can be related to what follows. Faster readers use anticipatory scanning techniques looking ahead in the material to predict the nature of material they have not yet read.

Concentration

Slow readers often lack concentration except for short periods. Efficient readers concentrate well by excluding distractions, reading at times of day when they know from experience they can concentrate better and reading in environments conducive to good concentration.

Retention

Inefficient readers are frequently unable to retain information for very long after reading. Faster readers tend to have good retention of information over longer periods because they use the kinds of techniques we shall be discussing in Chapter 6.

Purpose

Slow readers are unsure about their purposes in reading which means they have no clear goals to aim for when they read. Faster readers make sure that they have a clear knowledge of their purpose and expectations before they begin to read something.

EDUCATIONAL DIFFERENCES

The last group of differences we might call education or cultural. They are difficult to improve in a fairly short programme like the one in this book, but they can be improved in the longer term.

Vocabulary

Vocabulary is a significant factor in reading. The broader your vocabulary, the better. You can build it up systematically by keeping a notebook for new words encountered. Write in the dictionary definition and then try to use the words in sentences of your own construction. If possible, have someone check for you that you have understood the meaning and are using a word correctly. Most people have a partner or a friend who will do this for them.

Background knowledge

Another factor is your general background of knowledge and experience. The broader this is, the more likely you are to be able to tackle materials of greater difficulty drawn from a wider range of subject areas. Breadth of scope breeds more breadth as well as greater depth of understanding.

Reading critically

Slow readers are unable to read critically, in the sense of not just looking for faults, but looking for points of merit as well. Faster readers can do this without loss of speed by using the type of strategy we shall look at in the next chapter.

LEARNING TECHNIQUES TO ADDRESS THESE PROBLEMS

The practical consequences of these fourteen differences is that, if we can do what naturally efficient readers do as often as we can, we shall experience improvements not only in our speed of reading, but in the quality of our recall and comprehension as well.

Now let us see what we can do specifically by way of new techniques about the first group of differences discussed above.

No more regression

We know that regressions are a problem because they inevitably slow you down and contribute greatly to making reading a tedious and time-consuming chore. From this point on, therefore, there is to be no more regression. To prevent it, take a sheet of A4 paper and fold it in two. Fold it in two again so that it is approximately postcard shape and size. You may recall using a piece of paper or card when you were learning to read in primary school. You kept it underneath the line you were reading to prevent your eyes skipping from one line to another. Now you will use it in a different way. Place it above the line you are reading and draw it down to progressively cover the text you have read. Never move it upwards. Never let it stand still. Never bring it down about three lines behind where you are just in case. Try it now. Once you get used to it you should find that not only does your speed improve, often dramatically, but so does concentration. This is simply because you have to concentrate more when you are doing something new and still want to take in the meaning of what you read. You should read without regression for the rest of this programme, unless you are given different instructions.

Developing a rhythm

Try to develop a rhythm as you practise avoiding regression. Avoiding regression creates a rhythm in the first place and getting into a rhythm helps to prevent regressions because we do not like to break a rhythm once established.

Making better use of eye span

Now, how can we make better use of our available eye span? There are, as we said earlier, three techniques for you to try and see which works best for you.

- Instead of looking at every word, try looking at alternate words. If you can do it, it will clearly instantly double your reading speed.

- If that does not work, try to identify groups of words rather than single words. Even in a simple sentence like 'The quick brown fox jumps over the lazy dog' words group together. 'The quick brown fox' is one group, 'jumps over' is another and 'the lazy dog' is a third. If this works, it can more than double your reading speed.

- If neither of these techniques works for you, simply try reading faster, something you should, of course, already be doing. Many people find this is the simplest and easiest way to get the brain to change the way it is prepared to accept information. Later, when you are reading faster, you can examine your technique again. If you are indeed reading faster, you will almost certainly notice that you are making fewer fixations and are therefore making better use of your available eye span.

Flashing

One other little technique for you to try – which was used for many years in programmes like this until people realised that it very rarely worked – is tachistoscopic practice or **flashing** as it is more popularly known.

You take your anti-regression device (the folded piece of paper) and select a column in a newspaper. Give yourself the first line, cover up the second and lower few lines. Then pull the piece of paper down and return it up to its original position as quickly as you physically can. Write down what you have seen 'flashed' before your eyes. Do this for ten or twenty lines. If it happens to work for you, it will help to widen your use of your eye span. If it does not work, do not worry. It very rarely does, but it is at least worth trying it out once.

EXERCISE

Now read the following exercise, concentrating particularly on not regressing as you read and on trying for a new personal best for speed and comprehension.

Start timing and begin reading NOW.

It Never Rains But It Pours

After quite a reasonable summer with quite pleasant periods of warm sunshine and less than average rainfall, the autumn turned out to be very different. From the beginning of October it became noticeably colder and a great deal wetter. The rain continued for days at a time and for the last two weeks of the month it rained steadily. This was accompanied by very high winds and caused widespread damage to buildings and serious flooding. All parts of the country were affected, but conditions were particularly bad in the South East.

At International Consolidated Insurance Group, claims began to arrive towards the end of October and rose sharply in the early part of November. There were so many that the staff found it impossible to investigate each claim as thoroughly as they would like. As part of company policy, the view was taken to pay up and ask questions afterwards. This was seen as contributing to good customer relations and an appropriate response to a government plea to insurance companies to do as much as they could to assist, in particular, hard hit householders whose properties had been damaged.

There were so many claims that there was a natural suspicion that not all of them were genuine. Towards the end of November, when the weather had improved and the winds and the floods had subsided, the number of claims received declined steadily and staff were able to give each one more careful attention.

One in particular caught the attention of Geoffrey Fairhurst. It came from a Mr Bernard Atherton in Sunderland. By chance, Geoffrey had been born in Sunderland and had spent much of his early life there before his parents moved south in search of work when shipbuilding began to decline. He knew the area well and he knew the part of the city in which Mr Atherton lived especially well as he had had an early girl friend living in the vicinity.

Mr Atherton had claimed £1250 for damage to his property caused by flooding. On the face of it, the claim looked reasonable as the east coast had suffered almost as badly as the South East. Geoffrey, however, was doubtful for a reason he could not at first define. The claim was made out properly. There was a receipt from a local builder approved by the company detailing the work that had had to be done together with the reasons for it. Yet Geoffrey was not happy with the claim. He pored over it for some time, but still could not identify precisely what was puzzling him. At length, he put it to one side and turned to other claims.

He was checking the details of a claim made from Hillcrest Avenue in Hull when it suddenly came to him. It lay in the juxtaposition of Hillcrest and Hull for he thought it odd to have a street labelled Hillcrest in a city that was known for its flatness, a fact demonstrated in the old days by the number of cycles per head of population. At one time it reputedly had more than Copenhagen.

Of course, he told himself, that was it: the hill. He remembered that the part of Sunderland in which Mr Atherton lived was on a hill. Indeed, Mr Atherton's address, Geoffrey recalled, was almost at the top of the hill. It did not seem a likely place for a flood to strike. Consequently, he marked the file as one for the company's investigators to enquire into.

This was duly done and the report came back that there had in fact been damage to the property, but it had been caused by the high winds and not flooding. It further transpired that Mr Atherton was an elderly gentleman whose eyesight was not as good as it once was. He had, however, submitted a false claim.

It also emerged that, on investigation, a number of claims from that part of the North East contained similar errors. The builders, meanwhile, had ceased trading and the owners could not be traced. Local rumour had it that, having cashed heavily in on the claims made with their support, they had departed for the sunnier climate of Northern Cyprus until matters at home had cooled down sufficiently to permit a safe return.

(710 words)

Questions

1. When did the pleasant summer weather change?

2. Which part of the country was worst affected by the floods?

3. What prompted Geoffrey's parents to move south?

4. Why did Geoffrey know the part of the city in which Mr Atherton lived particularly well?

5. How much had Mr Atherton claimed for damage to his property?

6. What was the name of the street which caused Geoffrey to realise what was suspicious about Mr Atherton's claim?

7. Hull had once reputedly had more cycles per head of population than which city?

8. What had caused the damage to Mr Atherton's property?

9. What was the status of the builders now?

10. Where were the builders now?

Convert the reading time into words per minute (using the conversion table on pages 119–120), check the answers to the recall test against the answers on pages 121–122 and record both results on the progress graphs on page 120.

ASSESSMENT OF RESULTS

Many people find that simply by avoiding regressions they get a dramatic increase in reading speed. If you did, that is good. If you didn't, don't worry. Keep trying.

You may experience some loss of comprehension at first. This is quite normal. It happens simply because you are reading in a different way from the way you are used to. As with many of the techniques in this programme, you have to establish a new position, as it were, and then you have to consolidate it with practice. You have to become familiar with the new technique. Familiarity, in this context, breeds comprehension.

FURTHER PRACTICE

Select from the pile of unread items on your desk some that you know you ought to read but will probably otherwise never get around to reading. Use them to practise avoiding regressions. Time, test and record your results in the way described on pages 10–11.

CHAPTER SUMMARY

In this chapter you have learned:

- the nature of the reading process

- the 14 major differences between inefficient or slow readers and efficient or faster readers.

- how to avoid regressions when reading

- how to use more of your available eye span

- how to try tachistoscopic practice or 'flashing'

- what to do about subvocalisation.

5

Comprehension and Critical Reading

READING SPEED AND COMPREHENSION

It is important to remember that reading speed and comprehension are not two separate elements in the reading process, but two parts of the same thing. Reading speed clearly refers to the speed of reading comprehension. Comprehension rather confusingly refers not only to the whole process of reading but also more specifically to the quality of reading comprehension.

We use the terms 'reading speed' and 'comprehension' for convenience and we need to remember that each affects the other, though not always as we might suppose. For example, as you may already have found out, low speeds do not automatically give better comprehension and higher speeds do not automatically give poorer comprehension.

EFFECTIVE READING RATE

There is a way in which you can use the two pieces of information about reading speed and comprehension which you get at the end of each exercise to calculate a third element which you may find useful. This is what is known as the **Effective Reading Rate** (ERR). This is not the rate at which you are reading effectively, but the rate at which you are effectively reading, if you see the distinction.

The calculation is:

Reading speed (words per minute) × Questions score %
Example: 250 × 70% = 175 = Effective Reading Rate

Many people feel that it is a more reliable indicator of real progress than two separate results. For the ERR to rise, normally one of three things has to happen. Either the speed goes up and comprehension stays the same, or comprehension goes up and the speed stays the same, or they both go up.

You can, of course, get freak results where the speed goes up dramatically and comprehension drops alarmingly and yet the ERR is still higher. You can prevent this by building in a minimum acceptable comprehension score. I would suggest 60% or 70%, though you can set it where you like in the light of your own results. If the comprehension falls below the set figure, you do not do the calculation. It does not count. There is then a built-in incentive to achieve at least the minimum acceptable comprehension.

READING COMPREHENSION

Reading comprehension is a complex process which comprises the successful or unsuccessful use of many abilities. When we read, we should be able to recall information afterwards. What we can recall and how much we can recall depends on many factors, as we shall see in the next two chapters.

- We should be able to select the **important points** from what we have read and be able to draw **general conclusions**. We should look for **key words** and phrases. We should be able to differentiate between **fact** and **opinion**.

- We should be able to make **deductions**, draw **inferences**, be aware of **implications** and **interpret** information. That is to say, we should be able to distinguish between **denotative**, or surface or literal, meaning and **connotative**, or hidden or unstated, meaning. In other words, we should be able to read both along and between the lines.

- We need to **relate** what we have read to our prior knowledge and experience, to see it in **context**. That is why the wide and varied reading we discussed in the last chapter is so important.

- We should **evaluate** and **discuss** what we read with others. In this chapter, we shall encounter a simple but effective technique for evaluating material. We shall learn how to read critically even at speed, where critically means not just looking for faults, but looking for points of merit as well.

Much of this activity takes place anyway, of course, quite unconsciously, but reminding ourselves of what we need to be doing should help us to do it more effectively. A lot of what you are told in this book may be put down to common sense, but that does not make it any less valuable.

FACTORS AFFECTING COMPREHENSION

Of all the factors which can affect both the quantity and the quality of our comprehension the main ones would seem to be:

- speed of reading
- our purposes in reading
- the nature of the material
- the layout of the material
- the environment in which we are reading.

Speed
Speed can have an adverse effect upon comprehension if you go beyond certain limits. What those limits are will vary a great deal from person to person and from time to time. If you were to read the next exercise at twice your best speed so far, you might well expect some loss of comprehension and your expectations might well be fulfilled. If you try to increase your speeds gradually, this should not happen, or if it does it will only be temporary until you get used to reading faster.

Purpose
It is, of course, closely connected with our motivation for reading and our interest in reading the material. Where these are poor or non-existent, clarity of purpose can often create a degree of motivation and raise the level of interest slightly but significantly.

IMPROVING COMPREHENSION

You can improve the quantity and quality of your comprehension in three main ways.

- Firstly, you can improve it by **wide varied reading**, where variety is more important than volume.

- Secondly, you can improve it by **discussion**. In discussion, your comprehension is immediately either reinforced or rejected. If others agree with you and you have clearly understood what you were reading, this reinforces the impression the material makes and assists later recall. If others disagree with you and you have clearly misunderstood what you were reading, this is in a sense even better. You can add their understanding to replace and augment your own so that you emerge from the discussion with more than you went in with.

- Thirdly, you can improve it by **testing**. You might not notice improvement in the course of working through the exercises in this book because they are graded to offer a gently rising level of difficulty in an attempt to counter the effects of improving simply through practice. If you follow the Further Practice recommendations at the end of each chapter, then you should soon see and feel improvements taking place.

Self-testing: self-recitation

There are two simple techniques you can use for self-testing which, when used in combination, can be highly effective. They are known by various names. The first is often called **self-recitation** or simply recitation. Some readers will know it as 'the journalist's questions'. Others will recall it from Rudyard Kipling's little rhyme:

> I keep six honest serving men.
> They taught me all I knew.
> Their names are WHAT? and WHY? and WHEN?
> And HOW? and WHERE? and WHO?

Ask the question:	*You are automatically looking for:*
What?	Events, actions, things
Why?	Reasons, conclusions, deductions, inferences, implications, opinions
When?	Time factors
How?	Method or processes
Where?	Place or location details
Who?	Information about people

Mind mapping

Self-recitation works very well when used together with a technique commonly known as **mind mapping**. Some readers may call it a spidergram or spidergraph, others may call it a recall tree, yet others may know it simply as spray, scattered or patterned notes. It is basically an alternative to the method most people use for making notes, which is to create lists of points. Lists are very useful, but they do suffer from two possible disadvantages:

- There is always a tendency with a list to regard the items at the top as more important than the ones further down. There is a kind of **hierarchical** feel about a list.

- There is often difficulty in seeing **interrelationships** between items in the list if there are very many of them.

Mind mapping, or whatever you want to call it, overcomes problems like these by the simple device of starting from the middle of a page and working outwards in various directions rather than starting at the top and working downwards. In this way, similar items of information automatically group together. It is also often easier if you use the paper landscape (horizontal) style rather than the more usual portrait (vertical) style. See page 47.

USING QUESTIONS TO READ CRITICALLY

At this stage in the programme, you may well find that when you are reading the exercises you are trying to spot questions that might be asked in the tests. Try not to do this. Read for meaning, that is, to understand what you read. If you understand it, it should not matter what reasonable questions are asked, you should still be able to answer them. If you can successfully spot questions in advance, all this tells you is that you are a good spotter. Since no one else need see your results but you, it is far better to try to be as honest with yourself as it is possible to be.

If you do want questions to spot and if you also want to enhance your ability to read critically, you should use three key questions from the self-recitation list: WHAT?, WHY? and HOW?

- The question **WHAT?** focuses your attention on the **content** of what you read and raises other questions like: What does

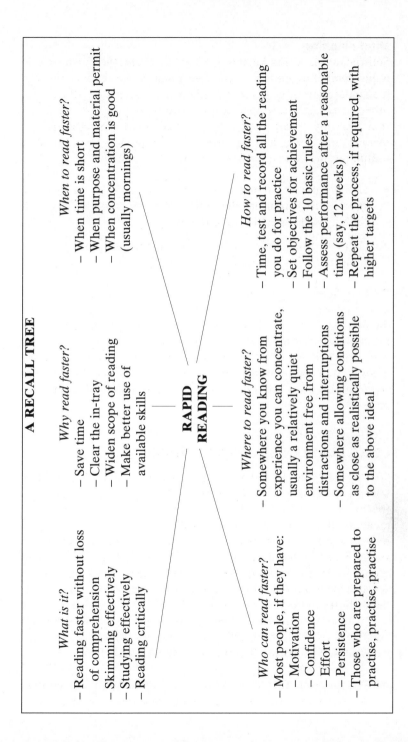

A RECALL TREE

What is it?
– Reading faster without loss of comprehension
– Skimming effectively
– Studying effectively
– Reading critically

Why read faster?
– Save time
– Clear the in-tray
– Widen scope of reading
– Make better use of available skills

When to read faster?
– When time is short
– When purpose and material permit
– When concentration is good (usually mornings)

RAPID READING

Who can read faster?
– Most people, if they have:
  – Motivation
  – Confidence
  – Effort
  – Persistence
– Those who are prepared to practise, practise, practise

Where to read faster?
– Somewhere you know from experience you can concentrate, usually a relatively quiet environment free from distractions and interruptions
– Somewhere allowing conditions as close as realistically possible to the above ideal

How to read faster?
– Time, test and record all the reading you do for practice
– Set objectives for achievement
– Follow the 10 basic rules
– Assess performance after a reasonable time (say, 12 weeks)
– Repeat the process, if required, with higher targets

this material tell me? Is the information accurate or plausible? What is the writer's authority for writing on this subject and is he or she reliable?

- **WHY?** directs your attention to the writer's **intentions** and prompts further questions like: What is the writer trying to achieve? Are his or her aims legitimate or worthwhile? You should compare the writer's purposes with your own. If there is no match, should you not be reading something more relevant instead?

- **HOW?** focuses on **treatment**. How has the material been put together and can you detect a clear, logical structure? This raises further questions like: Am I being convinced by reason or by appeals to emotion? Is there any evidence here of bias or distortion or concealment? Has the treatment influenced unduly my acceptance or rejection of what the writer is saying?

- A final question rounds things off: **HOW WELL**? This produces an **evaluation** of the material and leads to asking: If the writer fails, how, where and why does he or she fail? In the light of all these questions, or even of just the three key ones WHAT? WHY? and HOW?, what is my final evaluation?

EXERCISE

Now read the following exercise, concentrating particularly again on not regressing as you read and on trying for a new personal best for speed and comprehension.

Start timing and begin reading NOW.

The Missing Painting

Sam Marwick enjoyed his job as night security officer in the Department of Fine Arts at the University of Lochbrae. Of the people that he met, which were not too many since most had gone home by the time he arrived for his shift, he got on well with most of them. That did not include Professor Simkins, a rather severe and aloof personality.

It had all started when Sam tidied up some files in an office and put them into one of the filing cabinets for safety. That was his first week. What he did not realise, of course, was that some academics were not as security conscious as the people at the nuclear power station where he had worked previously. What he had also not realised was that the files belonged to Professor Simkins.

When the Professor came in the following morning, after Sam had left to get some well-earned sleep, there had been ructions. Everybody who ventured into the offices was accused of removing the files. No one could find them and it was only when Sam happened to come in early out of enthusiasm for his new job that the truth came to light. Sam remembered that interview he had had with the professor and had kept out of his way ever since.

This worked well until the painting of the Madonna and Child went missing. It was not a particularly famous or valuable treatment of the theme, but it had belonged to Professor Simkins before he donated it to the university. When Sam came in on the evening of the day on which its absence was discovered, he was met by Professor Simkins, Sarah Hill, his deputy, and Alan Jenkinson, the departmental secretary. What then ensued would have been described in politer circles as a full and frank discussion. What actually took place was a fierce and noisy row. The professor let his feelings about Sam's so-called incompetence come out in full clarity. Sam vented all the pent-up resentment he felt against the professor that had built up since the incident of the files. Sarah Hill tried to reason with them both, but simply achieved the result that they both turned on her and told her to shut up. Alan Jenkinson hovered indecisively in the background.

The upshot was that Sam stormed out threatening to go straight to his union, with the professor shouting for his immediate resignation.

The following day the painting mysteriously reappeared.

Sam confronted the professor and demanded an apology, which he did not get. He also demanded an enquiry to find out what had really happened to the painting. He did not get this either. Frustrated and bitter, he approached Sarah Hill for her support in making a complaint about the professor's attitude and behaviour, but she did not want to get involved and, clearly embarrassed, said that she had to support her superior. He got even less help from Alan Jenkinson because, search as he might, he could find no trace of him. He had, apparently, as it emerged later, turned tail and gone on a few days' leave (which he had suddenly remembered he was entitled to) to do some fishing in the highlands of Scotland.

Sam had no option but to withdraw to consider what his best course of action might be.

(550 words)

Questions

1. Who had a rather severe and aloof personality?

2. Why had Sam tidied up some files and put them in a filing cabinet?

3. Where had Sam Marwick worked prior to his job at the university?

4. What was the subject of the painting that went missing?

5. What took place on the evening of the day on which the painting went missing?

6. What happened on the following day?

7. What was Alan Jenkinson's position in the department?

8. Who did Sam approach for support in his dispute with the professor?

9. What was Alan Jenkinson intending to do when he was on leave?

10. What did Sam do when he withdrew from the situation?

Convert the reading time into words per minute (using the conversion table on pages 119–120), check the answers to the recall test against the answers on pages 121–122 and record both results on the progress graphs on page 120.

ASSESSMENT OF RESULTS

As we cover more ground and add to the list of points to bear in mind as you are reading, you may find that you reach a plateau for a time. If this result was not the best yet, you may find it helps when you do the Further Practice recommended below if you concentrate on the single most useful technique you have encountered so far. What has produced the biggest increase in reading speed? Build upon your success and work on that one technique in your practice before you attempt the next chapter.

FURTHER PRACTICE

Select an item from your 'slush' pile – those items on your desk you know you will otherwise never read – and follow these instructions very carefully.

Cover up the rest of the page below this paragraph before you read on. **DO THIS NOW**. Do not uncover the rest of the page until you have finished reading. Now read the item you have selected from your pile as quickly as you possibly can with no regard whatsoever for comprehension. Forget about it. Just read as quickly as you are physically able to move your eyes. Time it in the usual way and begin reading NOW.

Now, test your comprehension, using self-recitation and mind mapping. Did anything register after all, despite the fact that you were going purely for speed? It usually does and indicates that you still have potential to exploit. It also illustrates the fact that it is almost impossible to read something without gaining some comprehension of it. It is only a matter of practice to improve both the quantity and quality of that comprehension.

CHAPTER SUMMARY

In this chapter you have learned:

- that reading speed and comprehension are not two separate elements but two parts of the same process, reading comprehension

- how to calculate the Effective Reading Rate and what it means

- the nature of comprehension and the factors which affect it

- how to improve quantity and quality of comprehension

- the need to read for meaning, both denotative and connotative

- how to use self-recitation and mind mapping

- how to read critically and evaluate what you read.

6

Techniques of Retention

RETENTION IS NOT THE PROBLEM

The problem here is often not retention at all, but recall. We remember a great deal more than we realise. You must have had the experience of being asked for some information, the name of a person, say, and not being able to think of it, but as soon as someone else mentions the name you say, 'Of course, that's it.' This response indicates that the information was indeed available, but for some reason it was not accessible.

Our brains are capable of storing vast amounts of information about all manner of subjects, experiences, feelings and so on. Many older people, for example, can recall exactly where they were and what they were doing when President Kennedy was assassinated. Younger ones can remember the events of the hurricane in the south of England on 16 October 1987. You will have your own memories of significant events in your own life. My simply making the point may well have brought images not thought of for some time flooding back into your consciousness.

IMPROVING RETENTION: QUALITIES OF INFORMATION

Even though retention is not really the problem, there are still ways in which it can be improved. There are certain qualities that information needs to possess if we are to retain it more effectively. Many of them are based on simple common sense.

Meaningfulness
It helps to remember something if it possesses a degree of meaningfulness for us. It needs to have relevance. We do, of course, all remember a lot of useless information, which is handy for pub quizzes or playing Trivial Pursuit, but we remember much more that is useful. We should, therefore, first of all be clear about what the information means to us and how we shall use it.

Organisation

Information is easier to remember if it has a pattern of organisation, a structure. Often, because writers like to present things in a logical and ordered way, this pattern is easy to see. If it is not, we should look for a way of organising it ourselves. Mind mapping can be very useful as an intermediate step between material presented in a haphazard fashion and a point-by-point plan. Once similar items are grouped together on the mind map, all we then have to do is look for a sequence which suits us.

Associations

We should look for easy to remember associations between what we want to remember and what we readily remember already. These associations can then be linked together to produce patterns. Many people remember shopping lists like this. They know the layout of their local supermarket and can split it into areas. Their requirements can then be arranged to provide associations with those areas. They then produce a pattern of moving through the store which minimises the need to return to the same area more than once on a visit. If the supermarket reorganises its floor space, the process is simply repeated to suit the new pattern.

Visualisations

Visualisataions help us to remember things. If we can see them in our mind's eye and provide ourselves with a series of pictures it strengthens the impression made by the information. Even abstract concepts can be visualised. Democracy may be seen as a ballot being placed in a ballot box. Justice is often seen as a pair of scales.

Attention

Often we fail to remember because we have not been paying enough attention. We have not tried to remember. Effective retention does require a certain amount of concentration, though not so much that it causes us to frown with the effort. All that does is give you a pain between the eyes. The simplest way to deal with this point is, when you need to pay attention and concentrate, select a time and a place where you know from experience it is easier to achieve it. Most people find mornings better for tasks requiring concentration and conditions of relative quiet. Libraries or interview rooms without external windows are usually the most readily available locations.

Interest
A high level of interest in the subject matter and a strong motivation for remembering it help. This cannot always be achieved, but where it can we should exploit it to the full. Even uninteresting topics can be made easier to remember with motivation. Identify a clear reason for remembering. Chapter 6 will give you more on this point.

Feedback
Feedback is important. We need to check that we have indeed remembered what we want to remember. Self-recitation (see pages 45-46) enables us to gain this vital feedback. Always review it to make sure that there are no important gaps.

IMPROVING RETENTION: HELPFUL TECHNIQUES

In addition to these qualities that information should possess to make it easier to remember, there is a group of techniques which will offer further assistance.

Repetition
The impression made by information can be reinforced by repetition. Some things may need to be read more than once. Time saved on less important reading can be re-invested here to increase efficiency.

Discussion
Discussion helps to reinforce information. Most of us will have had the experience of going into a meeting having read and thought we understood all the papers only to find that others have seen things in them that we missed or misunderstood. We can then add their understanding to our own or modify it as required and emerge from the meeting with more than we went in with. Even if we have got it right in the first place, their agreement with us will still strengthen our retention. You cannot lose with discussion.

Writing things down

Writing things down helps. How often do you look up a new telephone number only to find you have forgotten the end of it before you can complete the dialling? Write the number down when found and, even without referring to it again, this does not happen. It has been reinforced.

Using the information

It helps, of course, if the information we wish to remember is actually used. If you don't use it, you lose it. Again, with telephone numbers, we are most likely to remember easily the ones we use. The one many people are most likely to forget is their own or at least part of it. Is it, for instance, 9342 or 9432? They don't use it much. Other people do. And do you know your car registration number? What about your driving licence or passport or National Insurance numbers?

Testing

Of all the advice given here, probably the single most useful technique for most people is self-recitation. It is surprising how much the simple act of getting into the habit of testing yourself on what you wish to remember and checking back with the original to confirm progressively increases the amount of information retained. Many of us have what we call poor memories simply because we are not prepared to invest a little time and effort on the activities in this and the next chapter.

EXERCISE

Now read the following exercise, concentrating particularly again on not regressing as you read and on trying for a new personal best for speed and comprehension.

Start timing and begin reading NOW.

One Not So Careful Lady Owner

Gridlock Insurance Services specialised in motor insurance. Whilse not being in the top ten insurance groups in the country, it had a fairly substantial list of clients and had a generally good reputation in the business. As one of the services it provided to its clients, it maintained a department whose primary function was to assist people in making claims against other insurers. This department was not large, consisting of ten young people with varying degrees of experience and expertise in insurance matters. This was not too critical as their main function was to expedite matters in the interests of their clients. In the event of encountering a problem with which they could not deal, they had a very experienced manager to turn to if they needed help with anything.

The department was a busy one and was becoming increasingly so. Up to now it had not let a client down by being unable to bring about a successful conclusion to a claim, but the growth of business made it increasingly likely that a mistake would be made. When it came, it came in the form of Mrs Armitage.

Actually, it came in the form of Mrs Armitage's son, Peter. Mrs Armitage had a rather old, but reasonably reliable, Ford Escort which was insured by Mr Armitage for any driver. In fact, the only people who used it were Mrs Armitage and Peter.

On the evening of Friday 7 May, Peter was using the car as Mr and Mrs Armitage had gone out with friends and, as they intended during the course of the evening to have a drink or two, had booked a taxi. Peter was out with his friend Roger and they had met other friends in the local supermarket car park. A crowd of young people gathered there most evenings after the store had shut and the shoppers and staff had gone home.

Later in the evening Peter and Roger decided to go to the local fish and chip shop for a bag of chips and jumbo sausage. They ate the food in the car, chatting as they did so. When they had finished, they put the wrappings dutifully in the bin provided outside the fish shop and prepared to leave.

As Peter was pulling out from his parking place at the side of the road, his car was hit by another driven by a young man of about Peter's age. The damage to both cars was surprisingly extensive and most of Peter's offside wing had virtually disintegrated. The other car involved, also a Ford Escort, was similarly damaged on the near side and, since it was considerably newer, would cost much more to repair if, indeed, the insurance company considered it was worth it.

The two boys exchanged insurance details and, as no one had suffered personal injury, the police were not called. They took down the names and addresses of several witnesses as the fish shop was quite busy at the time and the accident had occurred right outside. They then each made their way home as the cars, though badly damaged, were still driveable and neither had far to go.

When he got home and his parents returned Peter naturally received something of a roasting and a detailed grilling from his father as to the facts of the case. As they were quite satisfied, eventually, that it had not been Peter's fault, they went to bed.

The following day, Mrs Armitage contacted Gridlock Insurance Services and informed them of the details of the accident. They recommended informing the police in case there should prove to be any later dispute over the facts and asked her to complete and return the accident report form that had come with the insurance policy. This she duly did and waited for a reply.

When it came, the reply did not please her. According to the other driver, Peter had pulled out from the kerb without looking and without indicating. Peter denied this and set about the process of contacting witnesses. This proved an increasingly frustrating experience. It seemed that no two recollections of the accident were identical. A further complication was that the police had investigated and found a long skid mark at the scene, indicating that the other driver had, in fact, been speeding. The other driver denied this and claimed that the skid mark was already there when he came along. At least one witness statement seemed to confirm this. Peter and Roger, however, maintained that the other car had not only been speeding, but had been driving without lights. Unfortunately, there was no independent confirmation of this.

The matter was placed in the hands of the expediting department for their attention. They were particularly busy at the time and the situation was not helped by the fact that three people were off work with flu.

Several weeks passed and Mrs Armitage was becoming concerned about not hearing from Gridlock. She telephoned and the young man who answered promised to look into the matter and write to her as soon as possible. He was not a particularly experienced member of staff, the others were all busy and the head of the department was one of the ones who had flu. He contacted the other driver's insurance company and eventually negotiated a £250 write-off settlement from them. He wrote to Mrs Armitage accordingly.

Mrs Armitage was not pleased with the offer and wrote back asking him to approach the other insurance company again as she felt that her car, though old, was worth more than £250.

When her letter arrived, the young man had himself succumbed to the flu and was not at work. Those remaining were all too busy with their own caseload to attend to his. Two weeks later, when he returned to work, he found that the other insurance company had had a change of heart following a further letter from the other driver and were not now prepared to make any offer. They regarded it as a knock-for-knock case. He wrote to Mrs Armitage with the bad news. She by now was so angry that she wrote to the head of department. He had returned to work by now and asked the young man for a full report on the case.

(1055 words)

Questions

1. How many people were employed in the expediting department?

2. What was its primary function?

3. What make and model was Mrs Armitage's car?

4. Who actually used it?

5. For whom was it insured?

6. On which date did the accident occur?

7. What had Peter and Roger ordered from the fish shop?

8. Which part of Mrs Armitage's car was damaged in the accident?

9. What had the police found at the scene of the accident?

10. How much was Mrs Armitage originally offered in settlement by the other insurance company?

Convert the reading time into words per minute (using the conversion table on pages 119–120), check the answers to the recall test against the answers on pages 121–122 and record both results on the progress graphs on page 120.

ASSESSMENT OF RESULTS

If all is going well, you should be making steady progress by now and may well be a third of the way towards your target. Those who are doing particularly well may even consider raising the targets. If you are not doing as well as you would like yet, spend a little time revising the instruction in earlier chapters.

Ask yourself some questions. Are you really trying as hard as you might? Do you really want to increase your reading speed now that you know some effort is required? Are you still using your anti-regression device? Have you tried to reduce the number of fixations you make per line? Have you practised between studying each chapter? Are there any pieces of advice or instruction you have not yet tried?

FURTHER PRACTICE

Select an item from a 'News in Brief' column of a newspaper. Read it and time it in seconds. Put it on one side for half an hour. Now, using self-recitation and mind mapping, how much of it can you recall? Repeat the exercise with other items until you can recall at least 70% of the content or until you tire of it. You may even increase the interval between reading and testing to see what happens. At what point do you recall nothing at all? Does practice increase the amount of recall?

Count the number of words read on each item. there won't be many. Using a calculator, divide the number of words by the time taken in seconds and multiply by 60 to give words per minute. Check your recall by reference to the original. Divide the number of facts correctly recalled by the total number in the item and press the % key on your calculator. Keep a record of your results. Do they tend to improve with practice?

CHAPTER SUMMARY

In this chapter you have learned that:

- the problem is often not retention but recall

- the storage and retention of information can be improved

- for better retention, information needs to possess or be given qualities of meaningfulness, organisation, associations, visualisation, attention, interest, and feedback

- information needs to be reinforced by repetition, discussion, writing things down, using the information and testing.

7

Techniques for Recall

TRIGGERS

No matter how well information is stored, it will be no use to us if we cannot recall it readily. We must build triggers for recall into the storage process. Some, of course, are already in place simply through the way we have retained the information in the first place, but we can go further in this chapter. We shall look at a number of techniques specifically designed to ensure a greater degree of effective recall.

QUESTIONS

We have already encountered the use of questions in the storage process, but it is perhaps worth repeating here that questions in the form of self-recitation can be very useful in recalling information. The more you do it, the better you get.

MNEMONICS

There is a similar facility available to us in the techniques of mnemonics. Mnemonics is the name given both to the study of memory and to the techniques which enable us to use it more efffectively. There are eight main techniques and I shall explain them all in this chapter. They will not necessarily help you to read faster, but they should certainly help you to read more efficiently.

1. **Alliteration** or the repetition of a sound. For example, I remember being taught at school that the winter climate of the Mediterranean consists of 'warm wet winters with westerly winds'. You may be able to think of other examples.
2. **Acronyms** or words formed from the initial letters of the words we wish to remember. Examples would be SHAPE – Supreme Headquarters Allied Powers Europe – or HOMES – the five

great lakes in America: Huron, Ontario, Michigan, Erie, Superior.
3. **Acrostics** or the forming of a phrase or saying from the initial letters of the words you wish to remember. For example, 'Richard of York gave battle in vain' to remember the colours of the rainbow or spectrum – red, orange, yellow, green, blue, indigo and violet. Another one is 'Every good boy deserves favour' for the notes on the lines of a musical scale – E, G, B, D, F – with the FACE of the boy for the spaces between the lines.
4. **Rhymes** can be used to fix things in the mind. We have already encountered one in Rudyard Kipling's 'Six Honest Serving Men' rhyme for self-recitation on page 45.

Those, if you like, are the four easy ones. The remaining four require some practice to make them fully useful.

5. **'Loci'** is the name of a technique known to have been in use as a memory aid since at least 500 BC. (*Loci* is Latin for 'places'.) Roman orators used it to remember their speeches. They would picture their villa or a public building they knew very well and would set a path to tour the building. In each room they would make an association between the point they wished to make and something in the room. Then, as they were speaking, they would recall the tour and therefore recall the points in the right order. It worked then and it works now. Try it for yourself.
6. The **'link'** technique has been in use since at least the eighteenth century. It consists again of making associations and linking them together, but it can enable you to remember many more items. I once used it to remember the fifty states of America. There was no reason why I wanted to remember them, it was just an exercise. I took them in alphabetical order so the first one was Alabama. My association was the song 'I'm Alabammy bound' with a picture of a small train like the one in the Walt Disney film *Dumbo* on its way to Alabama on this occasion. The second one was Alaska so I had a picture of the dessert baked Alaska. The next task was to begin linking them together, so I had this picture of a trainload of baked Alaska on its way to Alabama and carried on from there.

I tried this one Saturday night as I was waiting for my wife to get ready for going out. So I had a couple of minutes to spare. That's the sexist remark out of the way. We went out, Sunday came and went and on the Monday afternoon I was in a meeting. It was a college academic board meeting and the only thing you know with certainty about meetings of teachers and lecturers is that they will always finish at four o'clock. They were all rambling on about something, probably car parking or catering, I can't remember, so I thought I would see how many of the fifty states I could still remember.

I still had 46 out of 50. I lost North and South Dakota. Well, if you lose one, you lose the other, don't you? It's like North and South Carolina. I also lost two of the states which begin with M – Minnesota and Montana. Alphabetical grouping was my back-up technique and there are eight states beginning with M, namely, working roughly from east to west, another visualisation back-up that sprang instantly to mind, Maine, Maryland, Massachusetts, Michigan, Minnesota, Missouri, Mississippi, Montana. So the technique did not work perfectly, but it worked a lot better than guesswork.

That is one problem with memorising techniques. They don't always work perfectly at first. But they do improve with practice. And they get faster. As we have said before in this book, once you know what to do, the rest is down to practice. Practice, practice, practice.

7. The **peg** system is a little simpler, but it is more limited. It is also based on the idea of making associations and linking them together, but this time in a set format. It begins by having certain rhyming associations with numbers:

        1 = bun
        2 = shoe
        3 = tree
        4 = door
        5 = hive
        6 = sticks
        7 = heaven
        8 = gate
        9 = wine
       10 = hen

You then make associations between the rhymes and the items you wish to remember. It works best with shopping lists. Let's say you wish to buy a water set. You picture it filled not with water but with buns. Secondly, you wish to buy a pen. You picture it as a shoe with the ball point sticking out of the end like a toe. Thirdly, you wish to buy a watch. You picture a tree with watches hanging from it instead of fruit, and so on.

You can extend the system by devising your own rhymes for further numbers. Twenty is about the maximum most people can handle with the peg system, but this is usually enough for many shopping lists.

8. The **phonetic** system is complicated, but it allegedly enables you to remember up to 10,000 separate items. Like the peg system, it is based on numbers and associations, but this time, according to many books on memory, sounds are incorporated as well, like this:

Number	Sound	How to remember them
1	td	t and d have one downward stroke
2	n	n has two downward strokes
3	m	m has three downward strokes
4	r	it's the last sound in four
5	l	it's Latin for fifty (ignore the 0)
6	g	upside down 6 looks like a g
7	k	capital K looks like two 7s back to back when written
8	fv	8 when hand-written looks like f
9	pb	p is a mirror image of 9 and b is 9 upside down
0	sz	the last sounds used for the system from the alphabet

The numbers then give various possible associations, like:

Number	Source	Examples
00	two s's or z's	zoos, seas, saws, shoes
01	s+t or d	suit, seed, sod, seat
02	s+n	sun, zone, sin, snow
03	s+m	sum, zoom, swim, seam
04	s+r	sore, soar, seer, sower
05	s+l	sail, seal, sale, soil

and so on for as long as you can find words to fit the numbers.

As I said, this is a very complicated system, but people have been using it since the seventeenth century. If you want to know more about it, refer to Kenneth L. Higbee's book in the Further Reading list. I can recommend it unreservedly. It is well written, highly informative and very entertaining. You will enjoy it as well as find it very useful.

EXERCISE

Now read the following exercise, concentrating particularly again on not regressing as you read and on trying for a new personal best for speed and comprehension.

Start timing and begin reading NOW.

One Gives Nothing So Freely As Advice

J. J. Jones & Sons Ltd is a medium-sized manufacturing firm in the Midlands. It makes components for the car industry and has recently been experiencing problems in keeping up with changes in the way that industry is run. In the old days, Jones' was able to make things in quantity and keep generous stocks of the items that its customers might require. As they were specialists and as they were usually given plenty of notice that an order was coming through, their delivery times and procedures were rather lax.

Since the whole industry moved to a just-in-time policy, however, they have experienced growing problems in meeting customers' demands. Some have transferred their business to other suppliers, sometimes leaving Jones' with numbers of items in stock for which there were no other likely customers. Over a period of time, the problem had become something of a crisis which clearly had to be tackled or J. J. Jones & Sons Ltd would be no more.

The management team was not a particularly young one. The managing director, Harold Jones, son of the company's founder, had been in post since his father's death twenty years previously. The finance director, Sam Prentice, had been in post for fifteen years, as had Arthur Locke, the production director. The other directors were the wives of the three men.

After a lengthy discussion at a board meeting, it was agreed to bring in a firm of consultants to examine the situation and make recommendations for action. As there was no money budgeted for this, Harold Jones decided to ask his friends at the local Conservative Club for advice on which firm might be the most suitable. He also let it be known that it would be helpful if they were also the cheapest.

Eventually, someone gave him the name of a contact at Consolidated Consultants who they thought might be able to help. Harold duly contacted the firm and they sent Brian Smith along to see him. He was an American, as were most of the consultants at Consolidated, even though the senior partners were all English.

Harold and the other directors explained the problem to Brian, who suggested that a team of three consultants with the relevant industrial expertise would be sufficient. As the investigation was to be carried out during July and August of that year and as the firm was rather lacking in business during the period, he offered an attractive pricing package. The directors of J. J. Jones & Co Ltd accepted it with enthusiasm.

Their enthusiasm, however, was to wane quite sharply at an early stage of the relationship. The sight of young people walking round the factory with stopwatches and clipboards did not please the workforce. Somehow word got around the industry that Jones' were in trouble. Orders dried up and credit was refused in several instances. Some of the best workers left for jobs elsewhere.

It seemed that the cure for the original problem was going to turn out to be worse than the disease.

(515 words)

Questions

1. Where is J. J. Jones & Co Ltd located?

2. How are their delivery procedures described?

3. What was the term used to describe the changed ordering policy in the car industry?

4. How long had Harold Jones, the managing director, been in post?

5. How many directors altogether were on the board of J. J. Jones & Co Ltd?

6. Where did Harold seek advice on which would be a suitable firm of consultants?

7. What was the name of the consultancy firm that was brought in?

8. What nationality were the senior partners of the consultants?

9. What event did not please the workforce?

10. Name one result of word getting round the industry that Jones' were in trouble?

Convert the reading time into words per minute (using the conversion table on pages 119–120), check the answers to the recall test against the answers on pages 121–122 and record both results on the progress graphs on page 120.

ASSESSMENT OF RESULTS

Hopefully, you will have continued your progress in speeding up your reading. Don't worry if you haven't. You might find it more rewarding at the moment to try to improve some of the memorising techniques discussed in this chapter and the last one. We have plenty of time to turn our attention back to speed before we have finished. At the moment, we might be better employed improving recall and comprehension. The next chapter should also help us in achieving this.

FURTHER PRACTICE

As you might already have expected, I recommend you spend the time between now and when you work on the next chapter trying out the memorising techniques. Have fun and delight your friends. Get them to set you some simple memorising tasks. Explain the techniques and get them to try them as well. You will find they work best if you do some before and after exercises: a task before you explain the 'secret' and a task after you have explained.

CHAPTER SUMMARY

In this chapter you have learned:

- the need to build in triggers for recall into the storage process

- the role of questions in recall as well as storage

- the role of mnemonics and how to use the techniques

- how to use alliteration, acronyms, acrostics and rhymes for simple recall

- how to use the loci, link, peg and phonetic systems for more complex recall tasks.

8

Flexible Reading Strategies

FLEXIBILITY – THE KEY TO READING EFFICIENTLY

If the programme is working for you, you should now be well on
the way to achieving your targets for both speed and comprehension. If it is working very well, you should on both counts be
ahead of your target lines. If it is not yet working as well as you
would wish, do not despair, there is still a while to go and there
are still techniques to come that may enable you to make the
breakthrough. You should by now at any rate have seen some
increase in your reading speed at least. Further practice will help
to improve comprehension scores.

Once there is an increase in reading speed, it is possible to
consider greater flexibility in using it. It is very difficult to be
flexible if you have nothing to be flexible with. If you have some
possibility of flexibility available, how should you use it? Clearly,
not every piece of reading material is of equal importance. You
should conserve your energies for more demanding material.

QUESTIONS TO PROMOTE FLEXIBILITY

To encourage flexibility, ask yourself:

- Am I spending enough, or too much, time reading this
  material?

- Am I taking enough, or too much care, over my reading on
  this occasion?

- Am I making enough, or too much, effort to understand what I
  am reading?

- Am I reading as quickly as my purpose, the material and
  conditions permit?

- Is there anything else I should be doing in order to read more
  efficiently?

- Am I ready to speed up or slow down if the material suddenly becomes easier or more difficult or if my purpose in reading it changes?

READING GEARS

The above questions will help you to make better use of the 'gears' or reading techniques available to you. I think the term 'gears' is a more appropriate one to use when you are talking about speeds. There are four gears:

- **Studying** involves reading, re-reading, making notes and revising. Undoubtedly, this takes time, but it takes less time when undertaken systematically. It is a technique to be reserved for those occasions when the content is difficult or unfamiliar or important and a high level of comprehension is required. A typical study speed is generally reckoned to be about 50 w.p.m., but this can rise to as high as 150 w.p.m. if some form of alphabetic shorthand is used in making notes.

- **Slow reading** is generally word-by-word reading and is what brought you to pick up this book or attend the course that is using it in the first place. It is usually accompanied, as we have seen, by a great deal of regression. Speeds run from about 150 w.p.m. to about 300 w.p.m., or twice as fast as the start of the range. 150 w.p.m. is a comfortable reading aloud speed. Radio talks are scripted at 150 w.p.m. and they don't exactly rush through those, do they? Even TV news scripts, though a little brisker, are only scripted at 3 words per second, which is 180 w.p.m.

- **Rapid reading** is the gear we are trying to get as far into as we can here. It involves groups-of-words-by-groups-of-words reading, largely without regressions. Speeds range from about 300 w.p.m. to about 800 w.p.m. though some authorities place the maximum higher than this. The late US President, John F. Kennedy, was reputed to read at 1200 w.p.m. Lady Thatcher is also said to read at the same figure. There is no sharp division at 300 w.p.m. You cannot say that at 299 w.p.m. you are a slow reader and at 301 w.p.m. welcome to the club, but the change in technique occurs somewhere around this area.

- **Skimming** involves allowing the eyes to move quickly across and down the page, not reading every group of words nor even every line. Skill in skimming depends on a clear sense of purpose, paying particular attention to headings and sub-headings, reading the first and perhaps also last sentences of paragraphs and looking for key words and phrases in the text. It gives you a general picture or 'overview' of the content, though it can be used to find specific information. Speeds usually range from about 600 w.p.m. (it can be lower if you were a very slow reader to begin with) to 60,000–80,000 w.p.m. These are clearly notional rather than actual speeds, but it can be surprising how much information can be picked up at quite high speeds. We shall return to a more detailed treatment of skimming in the next chapter.

USING THE GEARS

When would you use the various gears? Let us take some examples. Depending on your purpose and the nature of the material:

- You would use **studying** when the material is difficult and you need a high level of comprehension.

- You would use **slow reading** when the material is difficult but all you need is a general level of understanding or it is of average difficulty and you need a detailed understanding.

- You would use **rapid reading** when the material is difficult but all you need is an outline understanding or it is average and you want a general understanding or it is easy and you want a detailed understanding.

- You would use **skimming** when the material is average but you only need an outline understanding. You would also use it on easy material for a general understanding or an out-line.

STRATEGIES

It is highly desirable to build this use of the gears in reading speed into systematic approaches. There are several flexible reading strategies, as they are called, available. Let me suggest some for your consideration.

P2R

There are many occasions when 'reading' material three times can be better and quicker than reading it once. The approach usually known as P2R is one used by a lot of naturally rapid and efficient readers. It consists of the following steps:

1. **Preview** – skim for structure, main points, relevance, etc.

2. **Read** – as quickly as purposes and material will allow.

3. **Review** – skim to check that nothing has been overlooked and/or to reinforce points to be remembered.

It is not meant to be used rigidly, step by step all the time. Sometimes you will use all the steps. On other occasions, you will omit the first step because you are already familiar with the structure of the material. On other occasions, you will only use the preview and review steps because there does not appear to be anything new in the content so the preview will tell you this, but the review will be simply a quick check to be sure. Sometimes, you will decide to re-invest some of the time saved in this way in a second reading. There are several possible permutations, as you can see. Flexibility, as we have said, is the key.

S-D4

Secondly, there is S-D4 which works like this:

- **Survey** – a quick skim to identify the structure and the key points, then:
- **Decide** – one of four decisions:

    1. To skip, that is, not to read at all.
    2. To skim, probably at a slower speed than the original quick skim.
    3. To read at the appropriate speed.
    4. To study.

PACER

This approach is similar to P2R, but with more steps along the lines that we have considered in this book:

1. **Preview** – as before.

2. **Assess** – purpose and material.

3. **Choose** – the appropriate technique to use.

4. **Expedite** – a reminder to speed up again after being slowed down by a difficult part.

5. **Review** – as before.

Reviewing after reading should be undertaken with care. Remember it is only a skim. If you spend too long on it there is a danger that it can become a second reading. That would defeat the object of the exercise. It is simply designed to be a final check. If you really need a second reading, it is best to do it separately.

OTHER TECHNIQUES

Now for some additional points that will encourage flexibility and will also give you the opportunity to further increase your reading speed.

Taking risks

You should try to push the upper limit on speed as high as it will go, even if this leads to some loss of comprehension. You can after all go back at any time to slower speeds if you wish. None of the risks that you are encouraged to take in this programme will cause permanent brain damage. The option will always be open to set it all to one side and return to your old ways of doing things. But if you are prepared to take chances you will usually find that all that is required to make them work is practice.

Perhaps you may find it more acceptable if you try to read just a little faster than is comfortable. This will at least give some impetus towards improvement without becoming too stressful.

Reading fast, twice

Another technique which will be worth trying if material really does need to be read slowly at, say, 150 w.p.m., is to read it twice at 300 w.p.m. This will work very well if you use the first reading to understand what can be understood and make quick small marks in the margin with a pencil where there are problems. You can then use the second reading to deal with these problem areas, rubbing out the marginal marks as you resolve them.

This deliberate regression is preferable to regressing as you go along. If you fall back into that habit you will always be trying to resolve difficulties with an incomplete awareness of the context, until you get to the end of a passage. If you are going to regress, it is always better to do it after you have read through the whole piece first. That way you are able to bring to bear an awareness of the total context, which is bound to be more helpful.

Minimum reading speed

It is also worth trying to establish a minimum reading speed no matter what the material. I usually suggest a speed of 200 w.p.m. Nothing should be read at less than this. It is after all little faster than reading aloud (remember page 72) and it does help to avoid a situation in which you get two-thirds of the way down a page and have forgotten what you read at the top. This is nearly always caused by reading too slowly. The trace has faded on your mental radar screen and has to be renewed.

A little extra speed can also solve concentration problems. If you are one of those people who find that they are going along quite nicely and then, bing, suddenly they are on that beach in Barbados again – the eyes keep moving, but nothing is going in any longer – some speed will help to keep the mind on the task in hand.

Speed compels concentration. It is like driving a car. If you are on a completely clear motorway, say, the M25 at 8.30 a.m. (you wish), you still have to concentrate more if you are doing 70 m.p.h. than if you are doing 30 m.p.h. You are off the road that much quicker if you don't.

EXERCISE

Now, much of what we have been doing so far in this programme has been concerned with pushing our speeds up from below. This chapter and the next one will hopefully help us to lift our speeds up from above. We shall never lose the ability to read slowly when we want to or we have to, but we shall gain the power to read faster when required.

For the exercise in this chapter we return to our customary way of dealing with an exercise to see if a further increase in speed is still possible. Remember to try for a new personal best.

Start timing and begin reading NOW.

A Grey Day in Grayborough

Mr Lawrence Merchant of 17 Willow Lane, Grayborough, reported a pothole which had appeared in the highway outside his house and which he considered to be dangerous to passing vehicles. The report was received by Graham Lassiter, the Junior Clerk in the Engineer's Department, at 10.30 a.m. on 5 January 200X and he promised to have the area in question examined as soon as possible. The Highways Superintendent's office was some two miles away from the Engineer's office and Graham could not contact anyone before lunch time as all officers were out on site.

After his lunch in the canteen, Graham left the office in a hurry to meet some friends, whom he had promised to see some fifteen minutes earlier. Graham rushed so much that on the office steps he tripped and fell and found that he could not move his leg. An ambulance took Graham to hospital, where the doctors discovered that he had a broken leg. They therefore admitted him to hospital and told him that he would be off work for at least two months.

As no action had been taken, Lawrence Merchant again rang the Engineer's office on 12 January 200X and reported that, apart from no one repairing the highway, the pothole in question was getting larger and consequently more dangerous. This time the report was received by Lucy Norman, who also promised to report the matter to the appropriate section. Lucy immediately rang the Superintendent's office and reported the pothole, but passed on the address as 17 Billow Lane, which was on the opposite side of the town.

Obviously, when the Inspector visited Billow Lane two days later, no trace of a pothole could be found. The Inspector contacted Lucy Norman who said that Billow Lane was the address she had been given, but, as Lawrence Merchant's telephone number had not been given, there was no way of contacting him. Under the circumstances, the Inspector dropped the matter.

Another two weeks elapsed and poor Lawrence Merchant was becoming more frustrated. He again rang the Engineer's Department and Lucy answered the call. After listening to Lawrence Merchant's comments for three minutes, she apologised most profusely for her earlier error and promised to do whatever she could to have the complaint attended to as soon as possible. This time the inspection was made on the following day and the findings were very serious.

The Inspector discovered that an area of road approximately 30 yards long, for the whole width of the road, was breaking up in the vicinity of 17 Willow Lane and the only remedy was to completely re-lay the whole of this road section. He therefore recommended the re-laying of the road to the Highways Superintendent, but, as a temporary measure, the pothole outside No 17 must be repaired to make it safe.

The highway maintenance fund had almost been exhausted and there was no money available to re-lay the section of road, the cost of which had been estimated at £85,000. Special approval would have to be granted by the Highways Committee for the money to be made available and the next meeting was not to be held for three weeks.

The temporary restoration had been arranged and the tarmac gang visited the site in Willow Lane. A car was parked across the pothole and, after exhaustive enquiries at nearby houses, the foreman of the tarmac gang was unable to find the owner to move the car. The tarmac gang, therefore, moved to other urgent jobs and this work was moved down the list of priorities.

Unfortunately, Lawrence Merchant was not at home on the day the workmen called and, to his knowledge, no action had been taken on his complaint. He was so angry that he wrote to one of his local councillors, who in turn asked the Director of Engineering for a report on the matter.

(650 words)

Questions

1. Outside which address had the pothole appeared?

2. How far away was the Highways Superintendent's Office from the Engineer's Department?

3. How long would it be before Graham could return to work?

4. Who received the second report about the pothole?

5. What was the first thing the inspector did when he could not find the pothole?

6. How large an area of road was breaking up?

7. What was the estimated cost of the full repair to the road?

8. What prevented the tarmac gang from filling in the pothole?

9. How long was it going to be before the next meeting of the Highways Committee?

10. Who asked the Director of Engineering for a report on the matter?

Convert the reading time into words per minute (using the conversion table on pages 119–120), check the answers to the recall test against the answers on pages 121–122 and record both results on the progress graphs on page 120.

ASSESSMENT OF RESULTS

If you have followed the advice given in this chapter and taken a risk, you should have another increase in speed. If comprehension still needs to improve, spend a little more time than usual on the practice suggested below before you tackle the next chapter.

FURTHER PRACTICE

Select some pieces from the pile and practise some of the techniques suggested in this chapter. The pile should be smaller now than it was when you started this programme. If so, this is another useful indication of the progress you are making. Keep a record of your results and your reactions to trying out the techniques. Which ones work best for you? Build on those and do not worry too much about the ones that don't. We build on success. You can always try the others again sometime when you have the inclination. Remember that just because something doesn't work at first does not mean it will never work. Occasionally you have to be patient with yourself.

CHAPTER SUMMARY

In this chapter, you have learned:

- that flexibility is the key to efficiency in reading
- questions to ask to promote flexibility
- the reading gears or techniques available to you
- how to use your gears
- how to develop systematic approaches to reading by using flexible reading strategies.
- other techniques to raise the maximum speed available in reading
- that you need to take risks, but only when practising, to further increase speed
- about the concept of the minimum speed.

9

Skimming Strategies

SKIMMING TECHNIQUES

Skimming should not be confused with reading, but it is a valid and useful reading technique. It involves allowing the eyes to break away from line-by-line movements and move more freely across and down the page.

There are at least three ways of achieving this:

- **Sampling** takes the form of reading parts of the material rapidly in order to form an impression of the whole. It concentrates on the first sentence of each paragraph because this is where the key information in each paragraph is most likely to be.

- **Locating** is vertical reading. It does not look very vertical as the eyes are continually drawn over to the right. This is because the material is not printed vertically but horizontally from left to right. The eyes then have to correct for this by moving diagonally to the left. So you get a zigzag pattern of eye movements which is further complicated by the fact that this kind of skimming will only work really well if you have already identified key words and phrases and are actively looking for them. If they are there or if there is anything else which is relevant or of interest, your eyes will be drawn to that information. This happens because in addition to the area of close focus vision that we call eye span, there is **peripheral vision**. This keeps you alive out on the streets. You see a bus coming 'out of the corner of your eye' long before it can hit you and you take appropriate evasive action.

We use peripheral vision every time we get to the end of a line of print and make the return sweep to the beginning of the next line. You are looking at the right-hand side of the page and cannot see clearly what is on the left, but the brain can see it sufficiently clearly to direct the eyes accurately to the beginning of the next line. If this did not happen you would spend a lot of your reading time missing lines out or reading again lines already read. Headings, words in bold type or in italics and words which begin with capital letters all help to attract the attention of the brain and therefore of the eyes.

- **Previewing** is a combination of the first two techniques and uses both first sentences of paragraphs and peripheral vision to identify the salient points. It enables you to obtain an overview of the material before reading or rejecting it and can be a great time saver.

USING SKIMMING

Skimming therefore has many uses. You can use it:

- to gain an overview and see the pattern of organisation of material (previewing)
- to find specific information (locating)
- as a substitute for reading when time is short (sampling)
- as a means of defining purposes in reading (previewing)
- to assess the level of difficulty of material (sampling)
- to supplement other techniques (previewing)
- to decide whether or not to read and to help in the selection of material (sampling)
- in using dictionaries and handbooks (locating)
- in reading classified advertisements in newspapers (locating)
- in assessing the relevance of material to your immediate needs (previewing).

You may well be able to add other purposes and uses of your own to this list.

USING SKIMMING WITH OTHER TECHNIQUES

Skimming can be used in the P2R flexible reading strategy. A most effective combination in many reading situations at work is skimming (previewing) and rapid reading (300–800 w.p.m.), especially if skimming is used to sift and select what you are going to read.

EXERCISES

Now you should try the skimming exercises which follow. A number of additional points may emerge during this practice which we shall later attempt to combine into a general skimming strategy.

The first is a **locating exercise**. You will have one minute to find the answers to as many of the following questions as you can. Familiarise yourself with them before you begin. The best way is to write the numbers 1 to 10 on a separate sheet of paper together with a key word or short phrase. You can then refer to them quickly if you need to without page turning.

Questions

1. What concept does the concept of development include?

2. Who has more claim to being a wealth creator than the industrialist?

3. Who is described as 'a wealth producer in a very real sense'?

4. What does the author say should happen to profit?

5. What is said to be 'one of the major concerns of any useful economic development process at the present time'?

6. What is one of the main things that needs to be done in any viable programme of economic development?

7. What is an incubation period?

8. When is success more likely in any activity?

9. What is the fourth step in the strategy for economic development?

10. Will the same methods work equally well at all levels?

As you find the answers to these questions, do not write anything down. Simply put the number of the question in the margin next to where you think the answer is. Begin timing or get someone else to time you. Remember you only have one minute. Begin NOW.

THE NATURE OF ECONOMIC DEVELOPMENT

Introduction
An economy, at whatever level from the community to the nation, can be said to be developing when it is growing. The concept of development includes the concept of growth. If an economy changes but does not grow, that cannot be described as development. Economic development, therefore, is concerned with identifying and exploiting ways of introducing growth into the economy. This can be achieved in a number of ways, as we shall see.

Wealth creation
The primary task is the creation of wealth, because unless additional wealth is created growth cannot take place. The key word, then, is 'creation'. Recycling or reprocessing the 'old' wealth (that is, the wealth which already exists) will not result in economic development, though it could conceivably result in economic change.

Wealth is created through work. It is often said that our industries are the source of our wealth creation, but this is taking too narrow a view of the meaning of the term 'work'. The research scientist has more claim to being a wealth creator than the industrialist, because without the efforts of the research scientist the industrialist would have nothing to manufacture. We need, therefore, to broaden our conception of what is involved in the process of creating wealth.

Ideas are at the root of wealth creation. Someone had to have the idea that there might be deposits of oil under the North Sea before that great industry, which has supported our present economic survival, could ever have come into existence. Someone has to have the idea that there might just be a market for any new product before it can even get to the drawing board let alone into production. Someone has to have the idea of writing a book before any of the many people involved in book publishing and selling can have work to do. The writer is a primary producer in a very real sense.

Steps in the process of economic development
Once the idea has been formulated then and only then can

the rest of the processes in the development of products and services come into play. The product or service has to be designed. A prototype has to be made and tested and refined into a marketable commodity. The product or service has to be marketed and monitored and modified where necessary. It has to be sold in sufficient numbers in a capitalist system to make a profit. Profit has to be re-invested in the development of further ideas and the business has to grow. Once all this is happening, the process of economic development has begun.

There are many other steps to be taken, of course, including the provision of sufficient finance to fund the enterprise in the early loss-making days and the development of a sound business plan.

Job creation

It is not strictly necessary that, for wealth to be created, there should also be the creation of jobs, but that is certainly one of the major concerns of any useful economic development process at the present time. It is a fundamental part of the thesis on which this article is based that economic development should have the creation of new jobs as a basic concern. I can see little point in it otherwise. More wealth without more involvement of more people in the creation of that wealth would simply exacerbate the present situation in which those who are in employment are getting richer whilst those who are not are getting poorer. It is no part of the purpose of this article to encourage the philosophy that 'unto them that hath shall it be given.' That path leads only to further social disillusionment, disruption and alienation. In my view, that is something which is not only morally repulsive, it is simply impractical. What is the point in creating a divided society in which, inevitably, there will be attempts by those who are deprived (or who claim to represent the deprived) to prevent the 'haves' from enjoying their wealth? It is far better to accept that wealth, when created, needs to be distributed fairly and to accept the basic right of every individual in a society to have a share in both contributing to it and in benefiting from it.

Improving the infrastructure

For this reason, one of the main things which needs to be done within any viable programme of economic development is an improvement of the social and economic infrastructure. It is necessary to establish the importance of infrastructure right at the start, if only because infrastructure is available to everyone. Improvements in it mean benefits for all of us. So we need to provide for high standards in such essentials as good transportation facilities (good roads and rail networks, good public transport, good freight services, and so on), good sewage systems, good housing, good working environments on business and industrial estates, and a whole host of other facilities which may reasonably be described as part of the infrastructure on which society depends for its proper functioning. This will not be cheap, but if we regard it as public investment rather than public spending we shall not only be nearer to the truth but also closer to appreciating that a well-developed infrastructure pays off in all kinds of synergic ways in the long term and even, in itself, promotes not only economic development but also social development.

The role of economic development in developed societies

We must at all times remind ourselves of the fact that economic development is an activity in which even highly developed societies need to engage in. The alternative is not merely economic stagnation but economic decline in relative and, ultimately, absolute terms. We need to have a strategy which will promote that process at whatever level from the smallest community or neighbourhood to the largest and greatest of nations. This is not to say that the same methods will work equally well at all levels. Clearly, adaptation will always be necessary to meet specific circumstances and to suit local conditions, but the overall strategy should work well at all levels.

A strategy for economic development

We need a strategy for economic development which includes the following stages and steps:

1. Preparation
Research to identify specific or local needs and opportunities. Collection and storage of as much information as is reasonably available about the economy as it currently is.
Establishment of the terms of reference for the economic development project or programme.
Definition of the objectives which the project or programme is to attempt to achieve.

2. Assessment
A systematic assessment of all the data acquired during the Preparation stage.
An incubation period (time set aside for everyone involved to mull over what has been discovered and decided so far).

3. Planning
A final decision on the nature of the project or programme to be undertaken.
Selection of the information acquired that is relevant to the project or programme.
The preparation of a detailed business plan of action to be taken.
The completion of all pre-implementation procedures.
Allowance for a further incubation period.

4. Execution
The carrying out of the work involved in the project or programme.
Continuous monitoring of performance and progress.
Adjustments in the light of the monitoring.
Completion of the project or programme (which may be in phases or stages).
Allowance for a further incubation period.

5. Review
A critical analysis of the project or programme in the light of the terms of reference and the objectives set.
An assessment of the success or failure of the project or programme.

The implementation of any necessary or possible modifications designed to increase its success.
Continuous monitoring of the project or programme after completion.
Moving into the Preparation stage for the next project or programme.

This basic strategy should provide a firm foundation for the conduct of economic development projects or programmes of any size and degree of complexity. Clearly, the more complex the programme, the greater the need for further refinements of the points listed above. Nevertheless, the contention here is that this structure will increase the success rate of economic development projects and programmes. Experience suggests that, whatever the activity, success is more likely to be achieved where people are working within a clearly defined and logical structure in which, for instance, they can see where they are (or should be) at any point in the process. This the strategy should enable them to do.

(1405 words)

In this next exercise you will not be looking for the answers to specific questions. The task this time is to see if you can identify the **salient points**. What are the most important things the document has to tell you?

You may well find self-recitation and mind mapping helpful after you have skimmed the passage. Make no notes during the time allowed, but you are free to make notes afterwards.

Once again you have one minute. Begin timing and begin NOW.

RESEARCH AND ECONOMIC DEVELOPMENT

Introduction
The first need in any economic development programme is for research. Before any plans or proposals can be formulated, there must be available an adequate information

base. Research is required into, for instance, the nature of the present industrial structure, manpower availability and markets for products and services. But that is only a beginning. Here we shall explore the nature of what is required and explain the techniques necessary for successful research to be undertaken.

Research as the basis for economic development

Research, then, is the basis on which everything else is built. Knowledge (or, in this case, information) is power and, in this context, this means the power to act effectively. Inadequate or inappropriate research increases the likelihood of failure. Conversely, the better the research, the better the prospects of success. Time and money spent in research is rarely wasted as it provides a sound bedrock for economic development. For these reasons, much of what follows here assumes the existence of an adequate research basis.

So, what kind of research is required? Most obviously, those who wish to promote economic development need access to databases which contain information about business and industrial organisations. If they are trying to identify indigenous companies which are capable of expansion, given the right kind of assistance, a database which covers local industry will be sufficient. Local authorities amongst other organisations often maintain these. If they are trying to identify companies which are expanding and which may be interested in moving into their neighbourhood, district, county or region, then a database covering companies in the targeted areas will be more useful.

Databases are, of course, maintained on computers, accessible through the Internet, or World Wide Web as it is often called, and it will therefore be advantageous, even necessary, to have at least one computer (in the case of very small, local or underdeveloped agencies) to gain access to them. But the availability of a computer, even a small personal computer, makes it possible to build up one's own databases. There are many software packages available which make the construction of a database a relatively simple matter. The storage of large amounts of information in a readily accessible form is thus a capability within the reach of even the smallest community economic development organisation.

Sources of commercial intelligence

If an organisation does decide to build up its own databases, and maybe even if it only uses others' databases, the kind of research it is likely to become involved in is perhaps better described as commercial intelligence. It will be necessary to collect, store and analyse information about companies, individuals, geographical areas and many other factors. Much of this may be obtained from directories, press reports and personal communication with people familiar with the local economy, amongst other sources.

When using established sources of information it is important not to overlook the obvious. It is all too easy to neglect the vast amount of information stored in the public library system, for instance. Conducting what are known as literature surveys, that is, finding out what has already been published about the local economy or the economy of the area from which inward investment is sought, can reveal a great deal of useful information. Then there are many standard reference books which can be worth consulting. An example might be *Who Owns Whom?* which contains details of the ownership of companies (this could be helpful in identifying who to approach in an organisation).

Other methods of research

In addition to the commercial intelligence kind of research, it may sometimes be useful to carry out formal research of the traditional kind. This may take the form of testing hypotheses about, say, the effects of different economic development policies, perhaps through the use of pilot projects. Then again, it may take the form of action research in which a systematic study is made of some development which is taking place in any particular case. For these purposes research designs will be required and, in this respect, it will be best to consult an appropriate university department.

Another method of research is to use surveys. For these to be successful and produce the kind of information on which effective action may be taken, they must be carefully designed. Questionnaires are not easy to construct and here again expert help, of the kind available in academic institutions, can prevent many problems from arising. The same is true for sample selection (that is, deciding who to send the questionnaire to) and the interpretation of results, among other things.

One rich source of research information which is often overlooked lies in the experience of others. Whatever economic development project is embarked upon it is unlikely that it has never been tried before. True, it is possible for unique and original approaches to be devised, but they are often rooted in some way in previous projects. Opportunities to visit and examine other economic development projects should not only be taken when they occur but should be actively sought. There is no point in reinventing the wheel, after all.

Pilot projects have been mentioned above and these can be useful ways of finding out whether or not an approach to economic development will work or not. Often it is possible to attract funding for such projects. Whereas many sources of finance are difficult to tap for established projects, the fact that a project is new or experimental seems to make it easier to open doors and unlock purses. They can also be attractive to the media who are fond of 'firsts' and the unusual. The resultant publicity may well bring in additional finance. Pilot projects must be carefully monitored and evaluated if they are to be of any real use and these procedures should be built in from the very beginning.

The chance factor
All of the above kinds of research require careful planning to be effective (we shall return to this point below), but there is one kind of research that requires little or nothing at all in the way of prior thought and preparation. That is, to allow for the possibility that chance factors may result in information becoming available. Chance encounters with industrialists who are about to make a relocation decision are the most common kind. Yet even here some preliminary planning is possible. Visiting an area known to have spawned inward investment in the past increases the chances of these kinds

of encounters occurring. So does atten[d]
exhibitions and business conventions. To [c]
given to those hesitant about whether to [b]
you certainly won't win a prize if you don'[t]

The role of academic institutions

The use of universities in research had already been
mentioned, but the importance of these institutions (and,
indeed, of colleges as well) in economic development means
that it is worth exploring the contribution they can make in
more detail. Academic institutions generally contain a wealth
of knowledge, expertise and facilities which business people
and industrialists often neglect, perhaps out of a suspicion of
'ivory towers' or out of ignorance of their true potential.

It should be remembered that these days many members
of staff of colleges and universities have themselves had
industrial experience and are thus familiar with the needs
of business. They can save many expensive mistakes being
made by, for example, giving advice on product design or by
providing facilities for prototype testing. The possibilities are
endless and it makes very good sense for those who are
interested in the economic development of an area to ensure
that academics and industrialists have facilities for regular
and systematic contact so that no opportunity for them to
work profitably together is overlooked. This integration of
economic development with further and higher education
may well be the key to the initiation of a project worth many
jobs and the generation of profit.

The establishment of this integration is beneficial to
both sides. Business and industry gain ideas, advice and
practical help, whilst the academic institutions gain valuable
updating experience, see industry as it really is and can
transfer theoretical knowledge into practical experience. No
one loses.

Sometimes an economic development project is too small
or too busy to conduct its own research. In such a case, it can
be done by academic institutions. But it can also be done
by others. Often consultants will carry out research for
small projects either out of a sense of social responsibility or
because it will provide them with experience in an area with

...ich they are not totally familiar. Naturally, in such circumstances charges will be reduced and may be waived altogether. It is at least a possibility worth considering.

Other 'helping' agencies

Then there are other 'helping' agencies to which it is possible to turn for research to be carried out. Promotional agencies in the regions will often do this if the prospects of employment or business generation are sufficiently attractive. Commercial sections in overseas consulates will often help in such activities as identifying likely contacts when visiting an area. Larger firms will often help smaller ones, especially if there is the possibility that out of it all there may be some possible benefit to the larger firm (there is, after all, no such thing as a free lunch). Big firms are often keen to help their suppliers, so this is another possibility worth considering. In one way or another it may be possible to 'piggy back' on a larger firm's research activities and benefit from their efforts. The prospects are at least worth investigating.

Some declining industries have set up agencies to help areas where jobs have been lost. They are well worth approaching even by those who are not exactly within such an area as in some cases their rules enable them to help people outside if the jobs created could be open to ex-workers in the industry. Last, but by no means least, there are Business Links, Training and Enterprise Councils and chambers of commerce which are all worth consulting.

The five stages in economic development research

Economic development agencies can encourage all these methods of getting research done by others, but they can also help people to do their own research. The process is not as difficult or as complicated as it might at first appear. It comprises five stages:

1. *Review* – assess the current situation from every possible angle, seeking especially to identify what is actually being done in economic development by both public and private organisations.

2. *Objectives* – having identified what is being done already, it is then necessary to decide what kinds of activities are desired and to set appropriate objectives for their achievement.

3. *Methods* – in this stage the available methods of securing economic development are reviewed and the selection is made of the techniques to be used in this particular programme.

4. *Evaluation* – there needs to be a built-in method of monitoring and evaluating the research which has been carried out and to do this at regular intervals during the process as well as at the end.

5. *Ongoing* – a decision needs to be taken on what research to do next once the current research programme has been completed.

The research department
One possibility that has not yet been considered but which some economic development projects, especially those of a district or county and larger size, may wish to explore is to set up one's own research department. This can be expensive, of course, as staff will need to be employed, but if the resources are available it could well be worthwhile. It has the advantage that all its efforts are dedicated to the success of the programme. It is clearly desirable to avoid duplicating what is already available because then resources can be directed into some other aspect of the project. There will be few, if any, economic development programmes which will not have more demands than their resources can satisfy.

(2000 words)

LEARNING THE LESSONS

Now that you have completed those exercises, what lessons have we learned? What techniques can we add to our skimming strategy to improve it? Let me suggest a general skimming strategy that you may find useful in future skimming tasks:

- To skim effectively you should first of all identify key words and/or questions you wish to have answered (self-recitation and mind mapping will help enormously here).

- Next, before you start to look for the information you want, you need to see how the material is organised, to identify the structure, using headings if available.

- Then you need to organise your key words and/or questions in the way the material is organised.

- Use headings and/or the beginnings of paragraphs to find the most likely places to look.

- Go looking in the most likely places first.

- Go for main points and structure before any details that are required.

- Repeat the process, if necessary, for any omissions (though this should not be the case if the strategy has worked as intended).

This will be a very effective strategy for most of the skimming situations you are likely to encounter. You will have the opportunity to try it out and to refine it in the exercises below in Further Practice.

ASSESSMENT OF RESULTS

This has not been like previous chapters. Clearly, you cannot record the results on these exercises on the progress graphs in the same way as you did in previous chapters but you should still keep a record in your notebook.

On average, you will have found the answers to five of the specific questions, where asked, and you will have identified about half of the main points, where requested. Anything better than this is good going.

FURTHER PRACTICE

From the pile, select some longer pieces (in excess of 1000 words approximately) and either have someone set you questions to answer or use the self-recitation questions to decide what to look for. Keep a record of your results in your notebook.

CHAPTER SUMMARY

In this chapter you have learned:

- what skimming is and how it can be used

- how it can be combined with other techniques

- how to use a skimming strategy which consists of the following steps:

  1. identify key words/questions

  2. see how material is organised

  3. organise key words/questions in the way the material is organised

  4. use headings/beginnings of paragraphs to find the most likely places for the information required

  5. go looking in the most likely places first

  6. go for main points and structure before any details required

  7. repeat the process for any omissions, though this should not be necessary if all goes well.

10

Problems in Reading

During the course of working through this programme you may well have encountered some problems. Problems with particular kinds of materials, problems with techniques and a whole host of other possible problems may have arisen. We cannot end our journey together without addressing some of these.

PROBLEMS WITH PARTICULAR KINDS OF MATERIALS

Newspapers

Most people read a daily newspaper. Some read several. Some have the *Financial Times* circulated at work. Many hotels give their business guests the *Daily Telegraph* every morning. Newspapers are hard to avoid.

- One problem with newspapers is the **bulk**. Take a look at the *Sunday Times* if you don't already take it. I have known people come on my courses simply because they were still reading the *Sunday Times* on a Thursday. What's the answer? Skimming. Use it to select what you will read. Read the opening few paragraphs. This will tell you if an item merits a full reading. Unless you are retired you will simply not have the time to read everything. Prioritise your reading. What do you really need to know? Once you have what you need to know, what would you like to know if there is time? What new fields would you like to explore? The arts, literature, history, business, politics, entertainment, innovations? The list is endless: the choice is yours.

- Many people have a problem with the **political bias** in newspapers. It is always there, declared or concealed, but it is not difficult to detect even where papers declare themselves independent of all political bias. The solution is to read more than one to obtain a balanced picture of the news. If you have never read the *Morning Star* (socialist, some would say communist), try it. If you have never read the *Daily Express* (right wing conservative), try it. You will notice the difference straightaway.

- Personally, I often **bypass the whole process** and listen to the World Radio Network on satellite or click into news services on the Net. If you are Sky subscriber or simply have a satellite dish or have computer access to a free internet service like Freeserve (all that costs is the price of a local telephone call), there is a wide variety of free radio channels available to you as well as the TV. Much of it is more interesting than the TV. So we have another lesson learned – you don't actually need to read at all to avail yourself of many sources of information. The catch is, of course, that you still have to use your own powers of critical analysis and common sense to decide what to believe. There is no way around that one.

- With newspapers, you may also have difficulty in finding **significant news** amongst a mass of triviality. Once again, strategic skimming will help. The more you practise and refine your skills, the better they will work.

Correspondence

One of the difficulties here is that there is often still a common use of outdated 'commercialese'. People tend to use very conventional, even old-fashioned and Victorian, forms of expression in letters. They write 'We are in receipt of your communication dated . . .' instead of 'Thank you for your letter of . . .' at the beginnings of letters and at the end they write 'Please do not hesitate to contact me if there is any further information that you require about . . .' instead of 'Please contact me if I can help further'. There are many other instances of such conventional and traditional phrases and the only reason anyone can advance for using them is 'That is the way we have always done it.' Some examples are shown in the box below.

Many letters seem to be reluctant to come to the point. There is frequently a lack of essential or relevant information and there is a good deal of insincerity and over-politeness. Consequently, many are much longer than they need to be. The solution would seem to be to skim for the central points. With most letters this will tell you where the letter has to go or what kind of answer or action is necessary. You read the letter in full only where that seems to be needed.

Old-fashioned	Plain English
. . . furnish all necessary particulars	. . . give details
I have endeavoured to ascertain	I have tried to find out
Awaiting your detailed instructions as to how you wish the goods to be supplied	As soon as we hear from you, we shall send the goods
Due to the fact that	Because
On the occasion of	When/on
In the event that	If
With regard to	About
In recognition of the fact that	As
With a view to	To
Enclosed herewith	Here is
Enclosed/attached please find	I enclose/I am sending with this letter
Awaiting the favour of your reply	I should be glad to hear from you

Journals and magazines

Journals and magazines bring with them the problem of bulk and frequency of publication. You have no sooner finished reading one month's circulation when the next arrives on your desk. There is also the problem of the range of material you are expected to be familiar with. The vocabulary is often wide or covers several specialised vocabularies. There may be bias in writers' presentations to support their own points of view on a topic. This has to be identified and accounted for in the reading of articles. Not all relevant information may be given as a certain amount of prior knowledge of the subject may be assumed.

I think you will find that skimming is once more the first step to get the overview. Then it can be useful to read the opening and closing few paragraphs. Top that off by looking for the salient points in the rest using the techniques of first and last sentence only of paragraphs that we have already discussed. Read in full only where necessary or desired.

Reports

With reports the problems are often rather more complicated. They can be bulky and there is much background material that has first to be absorbed. They are often not well written nor well constructed because they are produced by people who are professionals in their own field first and writers second and then only because they have to be. Many have never had any formal training in report writing. They begin their writing careers by finding a report someone else has written and then copy its format and style. Unfortunately, they often pick a bad report and then we are all in trouble.

Reports often have a wide circulation within organisations and as different departments need different information from reports this can make for a confused style which tries to help all yet helps no one. So what do we do with reports?

- Read the summary first. These days most report writers put a summary of the content at the front of the report. Logically you would expect a summary to be placed at the end as in the chapters of most textbooks. Since reports are designed more to be used than read, the most convenient place for a summary for the reader is at the beginning.

- You should then read the table of contents.

- Then skim the report as a whole, marking parts to return to.

- Concentrate on the main ideas and the logical development of the material.

- Re-read the selected parts, making your own notes if necessary, as, say, in preparation for a discussion on the report's findings.

- Important reports should be read with a pen or pencil and notebook to hand.

Legislation

Legislation present special problems. The language is often archaic and difficult to understand. The documents are frequently lengthy. The structure is different from most of the other documents you are likely to encounter in normal reading. Part of the problem, of course, is that most of us do not read a lot of legislation. We only read it when we have to. Perhaps the best solution is to read more of it. With practice comes familiarity. With familiarity comes greater skill in dealing with the material. This might sound like unpleasant advice, but maybe this is one case where it can be truly said, as say the athletes, 'No pain, no gain.'

Handwritten materials

Many people in the course of their work have to deal with handwritten materials. The basic problem here is legibility. Some people cannot even read their own writing. I know of no easy solution for those, like teachers and lecturers, who have to read a lot of manuscripts, especially around examinations time. An initial skim is always worth trying, but a better strategy may be to read the script more than once, the first time quickly taking in parts that are legible, then using the second reading to decipher the illegible. That way you will at least have an awareness of the total context to bring to bear upon the problems.

E-mail and teletext

A similar problem, though for different reasons, exists with e-mail and teletext. I can read fairly fast, certainly a lot faster than I used to be able to, but I cannot read material on video screens quickly. I am told that part of the problem is caused by screen flicker which reduces legibility and part by poor choice of colour combinations by those who prepare the text in the first place. I am currently typing on a notebook where the AC current is converted into DC current. It is much easier to read than text on my other computer which has screen flicker. That may give you your best answer to the problem.

Scientific papers

Unless you are an expert in the field, and sometimes even if you are, you will find that scientific papers are often poorly constructed, badly written and fail to differentiate fact from opinion. Skim them to decide whether or not they really are worth reading, use beginnings and ends of paragraphs as the most likely places for salient points, then read through the whole paper. It takes time, but it will save time in the long run, especially if you check your comprehension with self-recitation and mind mapping.

Committee papers

These pose a whole set of problems. Apart from being poorly constructed and written, there are just too many of them. I was a county councillor for many years and the volume of paperwork I was expected to process in a week was phenomenal. I think our postman was the happiest man in the world when a local government reorganisation abolished the council. As nearly always, skimming is the first step to select those items which do need thought and attention and which also may be contentious. Items which are for information only or which are already budgeted for or which are not important can be ignored and read later if there is no live football match on TV (or whatever your pleasure is).

Specifications

These bring problems in that they are very technical, very detailed and usually lengthy. You need to be an expert to read them. Expertise can be acquired through patience and practice. As with many of the documents that people find difficult to read, practice is the main salvation. Familiarity breeds comprehension in this context. It also breeds speed, but do not expect dramatic increases overnight. In the end a gradual increase is just as useful as a quick one.

Financial papers

For many people difficulties arise here because, by definition, much of the information is given in numbers rather than in words. Numbers are a different language. The best solution is to get the people who produce them to use pie charts, bar charts and graphs as much as possible. If they don't then you have to use an initial skim to try to produce your own picture of what the figures are trying to tell you. Again, practice makes this easier.

Contracts

The same applies to contracts. I am told by solicitors that they are easy to deal with and that you can tell by looking at a contract whether or not it contains things it should not or leaves out things which it should contain. Now there is a classic example of the importance of practice. Who reads more contracts than members of the legal profession? Hence, they know what to look for most of the time. No technique is perfect, of course, but perhaps one of the reasons that many of us have problems with contracts is that we do not read enough of them. Any author will also tell you that they soon learn to spot any changes to standard publishers' contracts.

Leisure reading

Most of this programme has been concerned with trying to solve reading problems encountered at work. Before we finish we should look at those found in leisure reading. What are they? Well, because you have unlimited freedom there is the problem of choice. What are you going to read? Do you decide to read fiction or non-fiction? How do you decide whether or not it is what you are looking for? How are you going to find the time to read materials that are not connected with work? The material, since you have selected it, will presumably be interesting because for leisure reading you will not pick items that are uninteresting, and the interest value may act as a brake upon speed. There may also be problems in evaluating the material. Is it good? Is it well structured? Is it well written? What is my overall assessment of the material?

- With **fiction**, try finding out something about the writer, especially if you like what she or he writes. Give reading a higher priority in your leisure activities. Try to read a fairly regular amount each week. Read both easy and more demanding materials. Evaluate them methodically, using the techniques we discussed in Chapter 5. Try to plan your reading. Choose at least one book a month and try to keep up with this reading programme. Concentrate on reading not only for pleasure but for deeper satisfaction as well.

- With **non-fiction**, to select the best book on a subject, skim several. Use the table of contents and any chapter summaries to help with this. Read the opening and closing paragraphs of chapters. It might also be useful to know the system by which your local library organises its book stock. Many libraries use the Dewey system and any librarian will show you how to use it. Books on rapid reading, for instance, are usually classified at 028.6, '0' being the general classification for books on communication. In most libraries it is situated nearest the librarian's desk. So, if you are looking for further practice in the skills we have discussed and where questions have already been set, you will not have far to go.

OTHER PROBLEM AREAS

Apart from problems with particular kinds of materials there are many others which may cause you concern.

Vocabulary

Do you have problems with vocabulary when you are reading? Do you encounter many words which you are not familiar with? It's a common enough problem and the answer lies in your own hands.

- Get yourself a **vocabulary notebook**. Make it out in three columns, the last one being a broad one. In the first column write the new word. In the second column write the dictionary definition. In the third write two or three sentences using the new word.

- Get someone who is good at English to check your work if you can. It may be that your partner can help. Many men find that their women partners are much better at English than they are. Don't ask me why. It's just a fact of life that females are usually better at verbal skills than males. Males are usually better at number skills than females. It's probably a cultural thing rather than a biological one, though nobody really knows. It need not bother us here. We simply take advantage of it if it is there.

Relaxation

Reading faster often makes you tense, nervous, irritable, de-pressed (to quote the old commercial). Try to take it a little easier. If this is not possible, try some physical relaxation exer-cises. You will find books in the library or your local bookshop that will help. Ther are also tapes that will tell you what to do (don't play them while driving, we don't want any unnecessary accidents).

Anticipation

Sometimes when you are reading it is difficult to anticipate what comes next. This often arises when the material has not been skimmed first. Never underestimate the importance of the initial skim. Use your anticipatory skimming techniques to the full. You know it makes sense, as they used to say.

Concentration

This is a very common problem. You are reading quite nicely and all of a sudden you are on that beach in Barbados or somewhere else in the world or thinking about another work-related problem. Your eyes keep moving along the lines but your mind is some-where else. The lights are on, but there is nobody home. This is, in my experience, nearly always caused by reading slower than the purpose and the material will permit. Push yourself just a little bit harder. This will force you to concentrate on the task in hand. As I said earlier, speed compels concentration.

Retention

If there are problems with retention of information, refer back to Chapters 6 and 7. There must be something there that will help. If not, try lying down. It sounds silly, but research shows that it works. For some reason people remember more and in more detail when they are lying down than when they are sitting or standing. That's why psychiatrists have couches.

Purpose

Sometimes the purpose is unclear in reading. If you find this is the case, your first recourse is to Chapter 8 of this book. If this does not work, pause for a moment and think. Regardless of all the advice you have been given up to this point, what do you really want from the material? How does this compare with what you really need? Are there any significant differences between the two? If so, what are they? A moment or so in contemplation may well provide the answer.

Motivation

Maybe your motivation for reading is not clear to you. You do need to be motivated to read well. You need to generate some interest at least in what you are reading. You can, of course, read without motivation. Many people with boring jobs do. But it helps to be motivated and interested. Interest affects people in different ways though. Some find that if they are interested they speed up. Others find that they slow down. I do. I find if I'm interested I forget about the clock. I start to read as if I were reading for pleasure. I have to keep reminding myself that there is a task here to be completed so I set a deadline. If you're like me you might care to try doing the same. If you find that interest speeds you up, you have no worries. A clear definition of purpose will see you through. Comprehension, on the other hand, is almost always improved by interest in the material.

WORKING THROUGH YOUR READING PILE

There is no exercise set for this chapter other than the usual Further Practice below. You should now be less interested in having exercises set for you and be working your way well down that pile on the desk. I would like to see you clear it altogether by the end of the programme. That would please me greatly.

FURTHER PRACTICE

Select items from the pile. You choose how many. Try to get a mixture of short items and long items, interesting items and uninteresting, easy to read and difficult to read. Try to use whichever of all the techniques we have considered that work best for you. Time your reading of each item. Use the self-recitation/mind mapping techniques to test comprehension. Keep a record of your results. If you can get someone to check them with you, so much the better. Basically, you are on your own now. We have to push you off the branch and see if you can fly. My best wishes go with you.

CHAPTER SUMMARY

In this chapter you have learned:

- how to deal with problems with particular kinds of materials, such as:
  - newspapers
  - correspondence
  - journals and magazines

- reports
- legislation
- handwritten material
- e-mail, etc.
- scientific papers
- committee papers
- specifications
- financial papers
- contracts
- leisure reading

- how to deal with other problems in reading like:
  - vocabulary deficits
  - relaxation
  - anticipation
  - concentration
  - retention
  - purpose
  - motivation.

11

The Finish Line

We have now reached the fourth stage of the programme: Evaluation. It is time to see if we have reached our destination. Have you achieved what you set out to achieve?

EXERCISES

You should read the following exercises in the manner with which we started (but, hopefully, a lot faster) to see how much improvement you have made.

Start timing and begin reading NOW.

Braking News

The Hoisin Motor Company has its headquarters in Seoul, South Korea. Its European operations are centred just outside Bridgetown in the North West of England. The main production plant is situated some one and a half miles from the M6 motorway, on to which there has been constructed a special access road for the company.

The factory has been in existence for nearly three years and production has risen steadily and currently stands at 50,000 cars a year. It is expected to rise to 100,000 within a further three years.

The company enjoys good relations with the local community and sponsors a number of local sporting and leisure activities, including the local football team, Bridgetown Bravados. It also contributes to several local charities.

Industrial relations are good and the local work force have adapted well to the oriental approach to management. Wage rates are among the highest in the area, which has no doubt been a helpful contributory factor.

Recently, however, there have been problems at the factory. Several cars have been returned to dealers shortly after delivery with purchasers complaining that the car did not feel safe during certain kinds of driving conditions, mainly when the roads were wet as a result of rain after a dry spell. People complained that the brakes had a spongy feel to them, had consequently to be pressed harder and then tended to lock which caused skidding. Dealers had examined the cars and could not identify a fault in the braking system.

Before the particular model had been launched, it had been subjected to all the usual tests and trials and had seemed to perform perfectly well. Engineers were baffled by the reported fault.

Clearly, something had to be done, but what? The various options were considered. It could be ignored, as the number of complaints was small and there had been no serious incident or accident as a result of the alleged fault. The cars could be recalled and examined to see if it was possible to identify the fault and correct it, but this would be very expensive and there was no guarantee of a solution being found. A warning could be issued to purchasers not to drive when it was raining, but this would produce incredulity in the minds of the car buying public and an extremely bad press which would damage, if not totally destroy, future sales. The car could be referred to engineers for further rigorous testing to see if they could isolate the cause of the problem. The design could be re-examined to see if a design fault was causing water to enter the braking system under certain unusual weather conditions.

All of the options were considered and discussed by the management team, but they failed to agree on which course of action to take. The situation was clearly unacceptable and the managing director had no alternative but to refer the matter to headquarters for advice. They responded by asking him for a report on the problem.

(500 words)

Questions

1. What was the name of the motor company?

2. How far was the main production plant from the M6?

3. How many cars are currently being produced in a year?

4. What is the name of the local football team?

5. Under what kind of weather conditions had some purchasers experienced problems in driving the cars?

6. How had engineers reacted to the reported fault?

7. What did the management team do about the problem?

8. What did the managing director do about the problem?

9. Where were the company's headquarters?

10. How long had the UK factory been in existence?

Convert the reading time into words per minute (using the conversion table on pages 119-120), check the answers to the recall test against the answers on pages 121-122 and record both results on the progress graphs on page 120.

Happy Pills

Pilobar Pharmaceuticals plc had a very good reputation in the trade for coming up with new drugs. It was an Austrian company originally, but now had laboratories in the USA, France, Spain and Great Britain. The British laboratory and production plant were based in a new town in the North East and provided employment for 2000 local people.

Some time ago one of the British scientists developed a drug which was originally intended for use in the treatment of a rare form of cancer which had previously proved itself resistant to most other known therapies. The drug was put through all the usual testing procedures and seemed to perform well. In fact it performed so well that it was rather hurried through the validation process in order to get it to the market as quickly as possible.

It had been on prescription for several months when reports began to come in of some unexpected reactions to the drug. A small number of people reported experiencing hallucinations after using it. These hallucinations, however, were not unpleasant and consisted in the main of feelings of extreme well-being, even euphoria.

No one became too concerned about this as not a single negative side effect had been reported and the drug did not appear to be addictive. It looked as if the company had invented what in pharmaceutical terms was the equivalent of being able to turn base metal into gold. Sales rocketed and profits soared.

One weekend, however, the production plant was broken into and all available stocks of the drug were stolen. It would take the company several weeks to replenish them and resume supplies to the market.

At this point two unexpected events occurred. People who had suddenly had their supplies interrupted rather than being taken off the drug under medical supervision became irritable, subject to violent mood swings and some became violent. One group of patients who lived locally even marched upon the production plant and demonstrated against the company. The demonstration became violent when the police tried to break it up and several patients and police were injured, some seriously. Secondly, supplies of the drug became available on the black market.

One of the illicit traders in the drug, in order to make his supplies stretch further, mixed the powder with ordinary household flour before processing it into pills. For some reason this changed the chemical properties of the drug and instead of inducing euphoria it now produced feelings of terror, nightmares and even suicidal tendencies. The company was thus faced with the problem of deciding whether or not they should resume production or whether it would be adequate if they simply improved security procedures at the plant.

(450 words)

Questions

1. Where was Pilobar Pharmaceuticals plc originally based?

2. How many people worked at the British plant?

3. For how long had the drug been on the market before reports began to come in of unexpected reactions?

4. What were these unexpected reactions?

5. How many negative side effects had been reported?

6. When was the production plant broken into?

7. How long was it going to take the company to replenish the stolen stocks?

8. What did one illicit trader mix with the drug?

9. What reactions did the drug then produce after mixing?

10. Apart from withdrawing the drug, what other option was open to the company?

Convert the reading time into words per minute (using the conversion table on pages 119-120), check the answers to the recall test against the answers on pages 121-122 and record both results on the progress graphs on page 120.

ASSESSMENT OF RESULTS

If all has gone well you should now be reading at twice the speed you started with and your comprehension should be better as well. This all depends, of course, on whether or not you have followed all the instructions throughout and done the recommended practice. If you still have some way to go to reach your targets, the answer is a simple one. You need more practice. You know by now what you have to do. You have the techniques. The rest is practice. Practice, practice, practice.

12

Continuation and Follow-up

CONTINUING TO IMPROVE

This is the fifth and final stage of the programme. We need now to consider how you are going to continue to develop the improvements you have made. There are several points you need to keep in mind.

- Firstly, you need to keep **practising**, for the next few weeks at least. Find some time every day – five minutes is better than none – for **TIMED, TESTED and RECORDED** practice in reading faster.

- Find some time each month for **general reading**. Read fiction and non-fiction, easy and more difficult materials. Your comprehension skills will gradually improve if they get variety and a certain amount of challenge.

- Make **periodic checks on your reading speed and comprehension**, using items from the pile on your desk and dealing with them in the way we have done all the mainstream exercises. Time them, use self-recitation and mind mapping to test them and do keep a record of all your results. This will provide you with continuous feedback on your performance.

- Periodically, it will be useful to revise the points made in the **Chapter Summaries**. That way you will be able to see if there is anything you have overlooked and may be able to identify things you have not done that you should have done.

- You should also do **follow-up tests**, using items from the pile, three months after working through the programme and also at six months and a year afterwards. After all, you are on your own now and you know what to do. You could, of course, use exercises from this book which you are sure you least remember, but often when you do that it is surprising how much springs back into mind. That, though, would be a useful demonstration of the point I made earlier that it is often not retention that is the problem but recall (see Chapter 6). You could make entries in your diary to remind you when to take these follow-up tests.

ONLY THE BEGINNING

In conclusion, I give you two bits of advice:

- Always keep the idea of improving your reading skills in mind.

- Do not allow yourself to think that your results at the end of this programme represent a final assessment. In many respects, you have only just begun to tackle the problems of improvement.

ABSTRACTS AND DIGESTS

There is one final technique you may care to consider. It comes in the form of a quotation from Francis Bacon, the man whom some allege wrote the works of Shakespeare. In his essay 'Of Studies', he wrote:

> Some Bookes are to be Tasted, Others to be Swallowed, and Some Few to be Chewed and Digested: that is, some Bookes are to be read onely in Parts; Others to be read but not Curiously: and some Few are to be read wholly and with Diligence and Attention. Some Bookes also may be read by Deputy, and Extracts made of them by Others.

The most useful piece of new advice from this is to consider the use of abstracts and digests. Most disciplines these days produce them. They can save a great deal of time in the search for information. Many are accessible on the Internet. If you have not already done so, you should explore them if you have the opportunity. Or you could get your local university to do it for you.

DELEGATION

There is also the possibility for those in managerial positions to delegate some of their reading to others. Why read it yourself if someone else can do it for you? That way, you will only receive the items that really matter and those who do the reading for you will gain knowledge and experience they might not otherwise get. Bacon, as long ago as the seventeenth century, though it worthwhile and that was long before the industrial revolution began to generate vast quantities of paperwork and long before the paperless office proved to be an illusion.

SELECTIVE READING

Remember the importance of continuing general reading. But read selectively as we said earlier. It is never a question of never mind the quality feel the width. Selection encourages flexibility and that is what you need.

REPEATING THE PROGRAMME

If you have not achieved the targets you set yourself at the beginning of the programme, and even if you have, you might repeat the programme in, say, one year's time. By then you should have forgotten most of the exercises and if you have kept your answers separate from the book, except for the progress graphs, you can construct new graphs.

BOOK SUMMARY

For your convenience, there now follows a summary of all the key points from the chapters in the book. This will save you having to flick through all the pages to identify the points you have to attend to and the things you have learned.

In this programme the key points you have learned are:

- How to measure your reading speed.

- How to test your recall of information.

- The structure of the programme.

- Your starting point for the programme.
- How to complete the first of the five stages of the programme.
- How to set objectives.
- How to mark them on the progress graphs.
- It is desirable to have additional aims and objectives.
- The difference between an aim and an objective.
- The need for self-competition and self-pacing.
- The need to try to read faster.
- It is important to persevere with the programme.
- The need to continue using techniques already in place.
- The value of time limits or deadlines for reading tasks.
- The role of motivation in training skills.
- The need to develop confidence in using the techniques.
- The desirability of having regular eye tests.
- The nature of the reading process.
- The 14 major differences between inefficient or slow readers and efficient or faster readers.
- How to avoid regressions when reading.
- How to use more of your available eye span.
- How to try tachistoscopic practice or 'flashing'.
- What to do about subvocalisation.
- That reading speed and comprehension are not two separate elements but two parts of the same process, reading comprehension.
- How to calculate the Effective Reading Rate and what it means.
- The nature of comprehension and the factors which affect it.
- How to improve quantity and quality of comprehension.

- The need to read for meaning, both denotative and connotative.

- How to use self-recitation and mind mapping.

- How to read critically and evaluate what you read.

- The problem is often not retention but recall.

- The storage and retention of information can be improved.

- For better retention, information needs to possess or be given qualities of meaningfulness, organisation, association, visualisation, attention, interest, and feedback.

- Information needs to be reinforced by repetition, discussion, writing things down, using the information and testing.

- The need to build in triggers for recall into the storage process.

- The role of questions in recall as well as storage.

- The role of mnemonics and how to use the techniques.

- How to use alliteration, acronyms, acrostics and rhymes for simple recall.

- How to use the loci, link, peg and phonetic systems for more complex recall tasks.

- Flexibility is the key to efficiency in reading.

- Questions to ask to promote flexibility.

- The reading gears or techniques available to you.

- How to use your gears.

- How to develop systematic approaches to reading by using flexible reading strategies.

- Other techniques to raise the maximum speed available in reading.

- You need to take risks, but only when practising, to further increase speed.

- The concept of the minimum speed.

- What skimming is and how it can be used.

- How it can be combined with other techniques.

- How to use a skimming strategy which consists of the following steps:
  1. identify key words/questions
  2. see how material is organised
  3. organise key words/questions in the way the material is organised
  4. use headings/beginnings of paragraphs to find the most likely places for the information required
  5. go looking in the most likely places first
  6. go for main points and structure before any details required
  7. repeat the process for any omissions, though this should not be necessary if all goes well.

- How to deal with problems with particular kinds of materials, such as:

  – newspapers
  – correspondence
  – journals and magazines
  – reports
  – legislation
  – handwritten material
  – e-mail, etc.
  – scientific papers
  – committee papers
  – specifications
  – financial papers
  – contracts
  – leisure reading.

- How to deal with other problems in reading like:

  – vocabulary deficits
  – relaxation
  – anticipation
  – concentration
  – retention
  – purpose
  – motivation.

- Always keep the idea of improving your reading skills in mind.

- Do not allow yourself to think that your results at the end of this programme represent a final assessment. In many respects, you have only just begun to tackle the problems of improvement.

13

Record Keeping

READING SPEED CONVERSION TABLE

						Number of words in passage							
	450	500	515	521	550	556	650	710	725	850	920	1055	1405	2000
Mins/secs														
0.30	900	1000	1030	1042	1100	1112	1300	1420	1450	1700	1840	2110	2810	4000
0.35	771	857	883	893	943	953	1114	1217	1243	1457	1577	1809	2409	3429
0.40	675	750	773	782	825	834	975	1065	1088	1275	1380	1583	2108	3000
0.45	600	667	687	695	733	741	867	947	967	1133	1227	1407	1873	2667
0.50	540	600	618	625	660	667	780	852	870	1020	1104	1266	1686	2400
0.55`	491	545	562	568	600	607	709	775	791	927	1004	1151	1533	2182
1.00	450	500	515	521	550	556	650	710	725	850	920	1055	1405	2000
1.05	415	462	475	481	508	513	600	655	669	785	849	974	1297	1846
1.10	386	429	441	447	471	477	557	609	621	729	789	904	1204	1714
1.15	360	400	412	417	440	445	520	568	580	680	736	844	1124	1600
1.20	338	375	386	391	413	417	488	533	544	638	690	791	1054	1500
1.25	318	353	364	368	388	392	459	501	512	600	649	745	992	1412
1.30	300	333	343	347	367	371	433	473	483	567	613	703	937	1333
1.35	284	316	325	329	347	351	411	448	458	537	581	666	887	1263
1.40	270	300	309	313	330	334	390	426	435	510	552	633	843	1200
1.45	257	286	294	298	314	318	371	406	414	486	526	603	803	1143
1.50	245	273	281	284	300	303	355	387	395	464	502	575	766	1091
1.55	235	261	269	272	287	290	339	370	378	443	480	550	733	1043
2.00	225	250	258	261	275	278	325	355	363	425	460	528	703	1000
2.05	216	240	247	250	264	267	312	341	348	408	442	506	674	960
2.10	208	231	238	240	254	257	300	328	335	392	425	487	648	923
2.15	200	222	229	232	244	247	289	316	322	378	409	469	624	889
2.20	193	214	221	223	236	238	279	304	311	364	394	452	602	857
2.25	186	207	213	216	228	230	269	294	300	352	381	437	581	828
2.30	180	200	206	208	220	222	260	284	290	340	368	422	562	800
2.35	174	194	199	202	213	215	252	275	281	329	356	408	544	774
2.40	169	188	193	195	206	209	244	266	272	319	345	396	527	750
2.45	164	182	187	189	200	202	236	258	264	309	335	384	511	727
2.50	159	176	182	184	194	196	229	251	256	300	325	372	496	706
2.55	154	171	177	179	189	191	223	243	249	291	315	362	482	686
3.00	150	167	172	174	183	185	217	237	242	283	307	352	468	667
3.10	142	158	163	165	174	176	205	224	229	268	291	333	444	632
3.20	135	150	155	156	165	167	195	213	218	255	276	317	422	600
3.30	129	143	147	149	157	159	186	203	207	243	263	301	401	571
3.40	123	136	140	142	150	152	177	194	198	232	251	288	383	545
3.50	117	130	134	136	143	145	170	185	189	222	240	275	367	522
4.00	113	125	129	130	138	139	163	178	181	213	230	264	351	500
4.10	108	120	124	125	132	133	156	170	174	204	221	253	337	480
4.20	104	115	119	120	127	128	150	164	167	196	212	243	324	462

4.30	100	111	114	116	122	124	144	158	161	189	204	234	312	444
4.40		107	110	112	118	119	139	152	155	182	197	226	301	429
4.50		103	107	108	114	115	134	147	150	176	190	218	291	414
5.00		100	103	104	110	111	130	142	145	170	184	211	281	400
5.15					105	106	124	135	138	162	175	201	268	381
5.30					100	101	118	129	132	155	167	192	255	364
5.45							113	123	126	148	160	183	244	348
6.00							108	118	121	142	153	176	234	333
6.30								109	112	131	142	162	216	308
7.00									104	121	131	151	201	286

PROGRESS GRAPHS

Comprehension

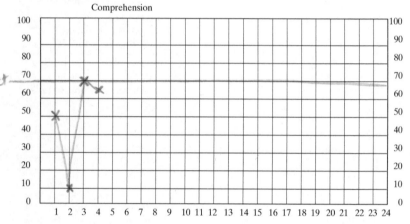

Speed ('words per minute' – see Table on page 119)

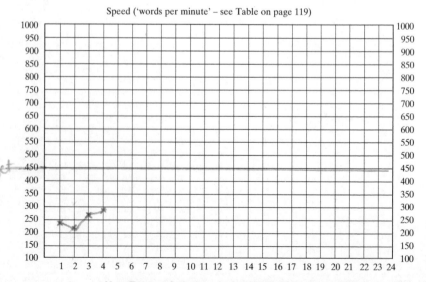

Note: Enter results in the order in which they have been read.

Answers to Questions

One of Our Tankers is Missing
1. James Wright
2. 2330
3. *Lady Lavinia*
4. Two years
5. Managing Director
6. Increasing incredulity
7. Ireland
8. Pretty good
9. Last month
10. Friday

If You're Going Back to San Francisco
1. Everybody's favourite city
2. Florida
3. Turk Murphy's
4. Pelican Inn
5. Bass
6. Highway 1
7. Santa Cruz
8. Los Altos
9. Bookshop
10. Geordie engineer

The Great Cash Register Mystery
1. Accountant
2. Susan
3. General dealer's
4. £1.20
5. Uneventful
6. TV engineer
7. Closed circuit television camera
8. Back of the till
9. Faulty spring clip
10. Mr Hobson

The Right Person
1. CFX plc
2. Call in consultants
3. He thought that people might think he was at fault
4. Head of Personnel
5. Last quarter's figures
6. The newest recruit
7. Two months
8. Fire drill
9. Interviews, assessment tests, practical tests
10. Mending a typewriter

It Never Rains But It Pours
1. Beginning of October
2. South East
3. Search for work when shipbuilding declined
4. He'd had an early girl friend there
5. £1250
6. Hillcrest Avenue
7. Copenhagen
8. High winds
9. Ceased trading
10. Northern Cyprus

The Missing Painting
1. Professor Simkins
2. For safety
3. Nuclear power station
4. Madonna and Child
5. A fierce and noisy row
6. The painting mysteriously reappeared
7. Departmental Secretary

8. Sarah Hill
9. Go fishing
10. Consider his best course of action

One Not So Careful Lady Owner
1. 10 (plus the manager)
2. To assist people in making claims against other insurers
3. Ford Escort
4. Mrs Armitage and Peter
5. Any driver
6. Friday 7 May
7. Jumbo sausage and chips
8. Offside wing
9. A long skid mark
10. £250

One Gives Nothing So Freely As Advice
1. Midlands
2. Lax
3. Just-in-time
3. 20 years
5. Six
6. Local Conservative Club
7. Consolidated Consultants
8. English
9. Sight of young people walking round the factory with stopwatches and clipboards
10. Orders dried up, credit was refused, some of the best workers left

A Grey Day in Grayborough
1. 17 Willow Lane
2. Two miles

3. Two months
4. Lucy Norman
5. Contact Lucy Norman
6. 30 yards long for the whole width of the road
7. £85,000
8. A car was parked over it
9. Three weeks
10. A councillor

Braking News
1. Hoisin
2. One and a half miles
3. 50,000
4. Bridgetown Bravados
5. Wet roads after a dry spell
6. They were baffled
7. Failed to agree
8. Referred it to headquarters for advice
9. Seoul, South Korea
10. Nearly three years

Happy Pills
1. Austria
2. 2000
3. Several months
4. Pleasant hallucinations
5. None
6. One weekend
7. Several weeks
8. Ordinary household flour
9. Terror, nightmares and even suicidal tendencies
10. Improve security procedures

Further Reading

21st Century Guide to Increasing Your Reading Speed, Laurie E. Rozakis, Ellen Lichtenstein (Dell Publishing, 1995).

How to Be a Rapid Reader, Kathryn Redway (National Textbook Co, 1991).

How to Increase Reading Speed, G. C. Ahuja, Pramila Ahuja (Stosins Inc, 1988).

Improving Reading Comprehension and Speed, Marcia J. Coman (National Textbook Co, 1997).

Mastering Speed Reading, Norman C. Maberty (New American Library, 1992).

The Photoreading Whole Mind System, Paul R. Scheele (Learning Strategies Corp, 1997).

Power Reading, Laurie E. Rosakis (Macmillan, 1995).

Rapid Reading in 5 Days, Joan Minninger (Berkeley Publishing Corp, 1994).

Rapid Reading Made Simple, Gordon Wainwright (Heinemann, 1972).

Speed Reading, Robert L. Zorn (Harper, 1995).

Speed Reading, Steve Moidel (Barrons Educational Series, 1998).

Speed Reading, Tony Buzan (David & Charles, 1988).

Speed Reading in Business, Joyce Turley (Kogan Page, 1990).

Speed Reading Made Easy, Nila Banton Smith (Warner Books, 1995).

Speed Reading the Easy Way, Marcus Conyers (Barrons Educational Series, 1998).

Steps to Reading Proficiency, Anne Dye Phillips (Wadsworth Publishing Co, 1987).

Time Manage Your Reading, Shirley Rudd (Gower, 1989).

Triple Your Reading Speed, Wade E. Cutler (Macmillan, 1993).

Your Memory: How it Works and How to Improve it, Kenneth L. Higbee (Piatkus, 1989).

Index